WONDERS OF MAN

Saint Lawrence, the third-century martyr to whom Philip II dedicated El Escorial

EL ESCORIAL

by Mary Cable

and the Editors
of the Newsweek Book Division

NEWSWEEK, New York

NEWSWEEK BOOK DIVISION

JOSEPH L. GARDNER   *Editor*

Janet Czarnetzki   *Art Director*

Edwin D. Bayrd, Jr.   *Associate Editor*

Laurie P. Phillips   *Picture Editor*

Eva Galan   *Assistant Editor*

Lynne H. Brown   *Copy Editor*

Russell Ash   *European Correspondent*

ALVIN GARFIN   *Publisher*

WONDERS OF MAN

MILTON GENDEL   *Consulting Editor*

1st Printing 1971
2nd Printing 1972
3rd Printing 1973
4th Printing 1978

ISBN: Clothbound Editon 0-88225-008-6
ISBN: Deluxe Edition 0-88225-009-4

Library of Congress Catalog Card No. 70-154726

Contents

*Detail of a sixteenth-century
vestment showing a gridiron,
the emblem of Saint Lawrence*

Among Juan de Herrera's many sketches of the Escorial under construction is this detailed cross-section of the basilica.

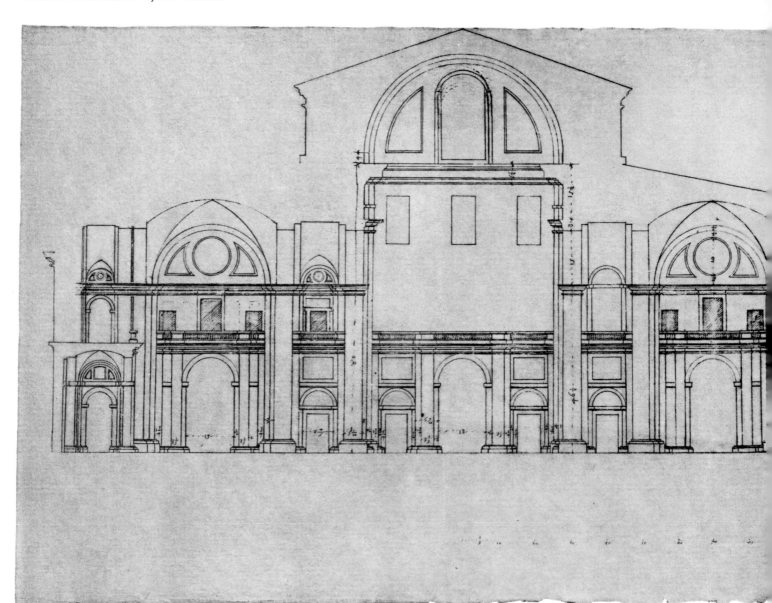

Introduction

As self-appointed champion of the Counter-Reformation, Philip II of Spain devoted much of his forty-two-year reign — and lavished a large portion of his seemingly inexhaustible supply of New World gold — on a foredoomed attempt to arrest the spread of Protestant heresies in Western Europe. The cost was staggering, the cause futile, and the legacy curious. For in his fervor Philip not only revitalized the infamous Spanish Inquisition, he also erected El Escorial, which has been called "an expression in stone of Catholicism in Spain; an answer, solid and unified, to the disintegration of the Christian universe." That sprawling granite edifice, set in the bleak Guadarrama Mountains, was physical proof of Spain's unwavering orthodoxy.

As the author of the following narrative indicates, the Escorial is more than a monument to the zeal of the Counter-Reformation; it is also a symbol of Spain at its imperial apogee. It was built to celebrate Spain's victory over the French at Saint-Quentin on August 10, 1557, the feast day of Saint Lawrence, a third-century martyr who was roasted to death on a gridiron. And, according to popular tradition, the Escorial takes its shape from Saint Lawrence's emblem — the enormous monastery-palace is laid out as a vast grid of intersecting corridors and interconnecting courtyards. At the heart of that grid is the austere Doric basilica of San Lorenzo el Real — and directly beneath the high altar of the church lie the remains of eleven Spanish kings, among them Philip II himself.

Unhappily, Philip's Bourbon successors were more interested in secular diversions than in sacred rites, and they neglected the Escorial for nearly a century. It was not until the last two decades — when the Patrimonio Nacional, a body of government-appointed overseers, undertook an extensive and costly program of renovation — that Philip's sprawling palace-tomb was restored to its former glory. Thanks to these efforts, modern visitors have little trouble understanding why Philip's contemporaries referred to the Escorial as *"la octava maravilla del mundo"* — "the eighth wonder of the world."

THE EDITORS

11

THE STORY OF
EL ESCORIAL

I

"A Dwelling for God on Earth"

Philip II, King of Spain, was dying. For years he had suffered from attacks of gout, but now, in the early summer of 1598, the pain was continual and he could scarcely bear to be touched or moved. There were ulcerating sores on his legs, and despite his physicians' continual bleedings, purges, and mysterious potions, the sores were showing signs of gangrene. Realizing that he had not long to live, Philip sent for his traveling chair and his usual elaborate retinue — for even on a journey toward death, Europe's mightiest monarch had to travel in suitable style. In June the king left Madrid, setting out across the wide plains for the slopes of the Guadarrama Mountains, where for years he had been preparing for himself one of the most imposing burial places ever seen.

Only his intense longing to die where he had planned to die enabled Philip to make the trip at all. The distance was some thirty miles and he had often ridden it in a day — but this time, carried slowly in a chair, and stopping frequently, he was seven agonizing days and nights on the road.

It was June, a month when the countryside should have been green with ripening fields and dotted with abundant flocks of fat, shorn sheep. Instead, the king saw only signs of extreme poverty and sorrow along the way: emaciated and ragged people, abandoned hovels, starving animals, and weeds where crops should have been growing. Spain, the richest and most powerful nation of the sixteenth-century world, was about to go into bankruptcy for the second time in forty years. Spain, whose armies were the best in Europe, had been at war continuously for almost three decades — first with the Dutch, then with the Turks, and finally with

the English and French — and by 1598 Castile had been bled white of her strong young men. These were tragic paradoxes, but then King Philip had known paradoxes all his life. Even his own personality was paradoxical, for he was simultaneously one of the most hated and most loved men in Europe.

On the afternoon of the seventh day of the dying monarch's final journey, the royal entourage came within sight of its destination: El Escorial, a huge parallelogram of granite rising against a background of forest and meadow, a work of architecture so sophisticated and so startling that a wayfarer who came upon it unexpectedly might have supposed it to be an unearthly vision. Indeed, Philip himself had called it "a dwelling for God on earth."

The king lived through that summer of 1598. Even in his extreme pain and weakness, he insisted on being carried one last time to every part of the Escorial. He knew it well, for he had watched over it closely during twenty-one years of construction. There were approximately 84 miles of corridors and courtyards; some 16 courts, 15 cloisters, 86 staircases; more than 2,000 windows and 1,200 doors — and most were like familiar faces to him. He was intimately acquainted with the church, the choir, the monastery, the royal tombs, the large collection of saintly relics, the infirmary, the sacristy, the gardens, the splendidly painted library, and the private rooms of the palace.

The whole constituted the most costly building in Europe; the equivalent of more than $45,000,000 — an enormous sum in those days — had been spent building and adorning it. But for the king himself there was only a modest suite of apartments and a very small bedroom from which a double door opened into the church. "He did not seem to come here as a king but as one of the severest monks," wrote one observer. When Philip had first planned the Escorial some forty years before, he had perhaps anticipated the time when he would be unable to rise from his bed in order to hear mass. And for the last weeks of his life the aperture between his bedroom and the church was the greatest comfort that his vast creation could afford him.

In order even to begin to understand Philip II of Spain, we need to look at the circumstances into which he was born in 1527. Much had happened in Spain in little more than fifty years, chiefly owing to the efforts of Philip's great-grandparents, Ferdinand of Aragon and Isabella of Castile (see genealogy, page 164). By their marriage in 1469 they had unified the two great rival states of Spain. Together they had pressured the Moors who had occupied southern Spain for more than seven centuries, and in 1492 they had succeeded in ousting the last Moorish ruler from his capital at Granada and exiling him across the Strait of Gibraltar.

Also in 1492 — and, as it developed, of greater significance — Isabella sponsored the explorations of the Genoese adventurer Christopher Columbus. The Castilian Isabella was more interested in overseas exploration than was Ferdinand, whose homeland of Aragon faced the Mediterranean and the Old World. Earlier Aragonese kings had conquered Sicily and Sardinia, and in 1492 a member of the House of Aragon sat upon the throne of Naples. Castilians, on the other hand, had been looking westward for years; earlier in the century they had conquered the Canary Islands. Most of Columbus's sailors were Castilians, while Cortes,

Pizarro, and many of the other *conquistadores* who soon set off to investigate and chart Spain's New World holdings, were from neighboring Extremadura.

Ferdinand and Isabella — known to history as the Catholic Kings, a title conferred upon them by Pope Alexander VI — may have had diverse interests overseas, but they were united in wanting more power for Spain. Since their own dynastic marriage had proved such a success, they set out to negotiate brilliant alliances for their children. Their eldest daughter, the Infanta Isabella, married the crown prince of Portugal; the Infanta Catherine of Aragon became the first wife of England's redoubtable Henry VIII; and the Infanta Juana and her brother, Don Juan, heir to the Spanish throne, married, respectively, Archduke Philip and Archduchess Margaret, son and daughter of Maximilian von Habsburg, the Holy Roman Emperor.

Fate was particularly unkind to Ferdinand and Isabella's offspring, however. Both Don Juan and Isabella died young, leaving children who died in infancy. Catherine, as is well known, failed to produce a surviving male heir to the English throne — and thus became the injured party in the world's most notorious divorce case. Juana's story was the saddest of all: married at the age of sixteen to the strikingly handsome Philip "the Fair" of Burgundy, she soon began to show signs of mental instability, a condition that was probably exacerbated by her growing desperation over Philip's faithlessness. Through her mother, Isabella, Juana was heiress to the crown of Castile, whose laws forbade the succession of the Aragonese Ferdinand. But before the queen died in 1504, she added to her will a proviso that Ferdinand should act as regent

Few political marriages in history have had greater impact upon contemporary events than the union of Ferdinand of Aragon and Isabella of Castile, who are seen in the 1490 painting at left, kneeling before the throne of the Virgin and flanked by two of their offspring. Wed secretly in 1469, the Catholic Kings ruled with verve and distinction for thirty-five pivotal years. In 1482 a native artist emblazoned the initials of Ferdinand and "Ysabella" (right) on the breviary of their unstable daughter Juana — and a decade later Columbus carried their crest to the New World.

should Juana "la Loca" (the Mad) prove unfit to govern. The following year, Ferdinand attempted to assume the regency, only to have his son-in-law adroitly step in and assume the Castilian crown as Philip I.

Philip's bold move might have led to the collapse of Spanish unity had the young man not died only a few months thereafter. Juana was inconsolable over her husband's death — and perhaps she was thoroughly mad, as contemporary chroniclers assert — but her story is so clouded by myth and gossip that after four centuries we can hardly do her justice. She is said to have displayed a shocking necrophilic interest in her husband's remains, opening the coffin time after time — but only two of these occasions are reliably documented. In any event, Juana lived the rest of her long life in forced seclusion. Ferdinand ruled her dominions until he died in 1516, at which time Charles, the eldest of Juana la Loca and Philip the Fair's five children, assumed the throne of a united Spain. Through his paternal inheritance, the youth was already ruler of Burgundy, the Low Countries, and Franche-Comté.

The Catholic Kings had certainly never intended to bring Spain into the sphere of the Habsburg family, but this is what had happened. Brought up at the Burgundian court, Charles spoke no Spanish and looked and behaved like a German — all of which got him off to a bad start in Spain. When he arrived to take over his new throne, he brought with him a large entourage of Flemings and Germans, whom he permitted to behave almost like a conquering army. He gave important government offices to many of them, ousting Spaniards in the process.

For his arrogance and tactlessness and, in particular, because he attempted to raise money in Castile to buy his election as Holy Roman Emperor, Charles soon had a full-fledged rebellion on his hands, one in which the Spanish nobility, the clergy, and the rich merchants united with the *comuneros,* the ordinary people of town and country, to oppose the crown. Fortunately for Charles, these strange bedfellows were unable to agree for long. The rich and noble soon began to fear that they stood to lose more from the revolutionary lower classes than from the despotic crown, and they deserted the *comuneros,* who were then crushed with ease and great severity by the king's armies.

Charles had many other, more difficult problems. His chief misfortune was in being too fortunate. His possessions were so vast and far-flung that they could not be readily governed — and Charles made the situation even more difficult by intriguing to be elected Holy Roman Emperor in 1519, when the death of Maximilian, his paternal grandfather, left that throne vacant. To win the election against Francis I of France, who was also determined to have the title, it was necessary to bribe the German princes who did the electing with vast sums that Charles could ill afford. Throughout his forty-year reign, Charles was continually short of money, and after the Netherlands and his Italian possessions had been squeezed dry, it was Castile that had to keep rescuing him from bankruptcy.

Having bought the election, the new emperor took the throne as Charles V (as King of Spain, he was Charles I). The position of Holy Roman Emperor brought with it more prestige than actual advantage, forcing Charles to concentrate troops and money in northern and central Europe, while neglecting Spain's

Led by such ruthless adventurers as Hernando Cortes and Francisco Pizarro, small bands of determined Spaniards subdued, enslaved, and systematically exterminated the Indian inhabitants of the New World. This 1540 illumination from a manuscript in the Escorial library depicts terror-struck natives fleeing the advancing conquistadores *(upper left-hand corner).*

interests in the Mediterranean and the New World.

The hemisphere opened by Columbus was being developed by eager subjects who often managed to evade any royal edicts that did not suit them. For example, although the crown strictly forbade the enslavement of the Indians, they were customarily subjected to "forced labor," and this practice soon brought the native peoples to the point of extinction. Administering and protecting such a vast and distant empire would have been a full-time job for any king. This one was vigorous, able, shrewd, and willing to learn from his mistakes, but as the historian Sir Charles Petrie has pointed out, "The trouble was that Charles had no time to do any one thing properly." He had to tackle whatever problem was most pressing at a given moment and muddle through elsewhere.

During the early years of Charles's reign, the westward expansion of the Ottoman Turks became alarming. This vigorous and warlike race from the steppes of Asia had been entrenched in the Balkans since the fourteenth century. In 1453 they had taken Constantinople, thus putting an end to the thousand-year-old Byzantine Empire and giving themselves a clean sweep of all the territory from Persia to the Mediterranean and northward to the borders of the Holy Roman Empire. At the time of the expulsion of the Moorish rulers from southern Spain, Queen Isabella had been in favor of following up the campaign with an all-out attack on North Africa. But at that particular moment, the Ottoman Empire was ruled by Bajazet II, a peaceable sultan, and Ferdinand had insisted that it would be enough merely to take several Turkish-held ports along the coast. A generation later, to Spanish dismay, the North

African coast was overrun by infidel pirates who made hit-and-run raids on Spanish ports and ships, harassed the Spanish-held cities of North Africa, and sold thousands of captured Spaniards into slavery. These pirates would almost certainly help the Turks if and when the Ottoman Empire should decide to expand toward Gibraltar. There was also a large, potentially traitorous Moorish population remaining in southern Spain.

Unfortunately for Spain, most of Europe enjoyed seeing her in trouble, from whatever source. France was her principal enemy and Francis I was more than a little uncomfortable at being encircled by Charles's possessions. When, in 1525, Charles dealt the French king a severe blow at the battle of Pavia, Francis began negotiations with the Turkish sultan, Suleiman the Magnificent. Eleven years later he went so far as to ally himself formally with Suleiman against the Habsburgs. Even the pope, fearing that Spain intended to deprive the Vatican of its temporal power and take over the Italian peninsula, carried on secret negotiations with the Sublime Porte (the Ottoman court). For the duration of his reign Charles was plagued by Suleiman and naval war between the Turks and Spaniards raged almost unabated in the Mediterranean.

Combating the infidel was a familiar activity for the Spaniards, but no sooner had Charles assumed his inheritance than a new kind of problem arose: in 1517 Martin Luther nailed his famous Ninety-five Theses to the church door in Wittenberg and signaled the Protestant Reformation. Eventually Protestantism was to prove the most trying of all the dilemmas faced by Charles and his son, Philip. But at the time of Philip's birth in 1527, it was still a relatively minor nuisance.

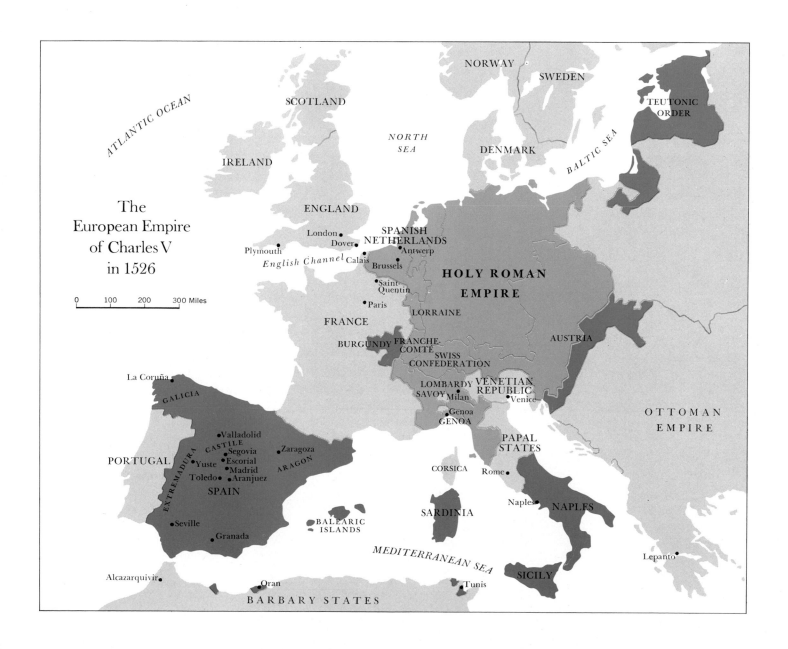

ATLANTIC OCEAN

NORWAY

SWEDEN

TEUTONIC
ORDER

SCOTLAND

NORTH
SEA

DENMARK

BALTIC SEA

IRELAND

ENGLAND

The
European Empire
of Charles V
in 1526

0   100   200   300 Miles

London
Dover
Plymouth
English Channel Calais
Brussels
Saint-
Quentin
Paris

FRANCE

SPANISH
NETHERLANDS
Antwerp

HOLY ROMAN
EMPIRE

LORRAINE

AUSTRIA

BURGUNDY FRANCHE-
COMTÉ
SWISS
CONFEDERATION

LOMBARDY VENETIAN
REPUBLIC
SAVOY Milan
Genoa Venice
GENOA

OTTOMAN
EMPIRE

La Coruña
GALICIA

Valladolid
CASTILE Segovia
Yuste Escorial Zaragoza
Madrid ARAGON
Toledo Aranjuez
SPAIN

PORTUGAL

EXTREMADURA

PAPAL
STATES

CORSICA Rome

Naples NAPLES

Seville
Granada

BALEARIC
ISLANDS

SARDINIA

MEDITERRANEAN SEA

Lepanto

SICILY

Alcazarquivir
Oran
Tunis
BARBARY STATES

As the delicately colored genealogical filigree at upper left suggests, Ferdinand and Isabella's successor, Charles V, could lay claim to virtually the whole of Western Europe. In administering his empire, Charles was obliged to suppress repeated threats to his authority; Titian's equestrian portrait of the bearded emperor (left) celebrates one such victory — over the Protestant princes at Mühlberg in 1547. During periods of domestic tranquility, Charles was able to indulge his appetite for large-scale hunts such as the one above. Executed by Lucas Cranach the Elder, the canvas features the energetic, black-clad emperor at lower left.

Philip, the only son of Charles and his empress, Isabella of Portugal, was born in the old Castilian city of Valladolid. In those days, Spain had no official capital, and the court still followed its medieval custom of moving from place to place. It happened to be in Valladolid when Isabella was brought to bed. Determined to show no sign of weakness during childbirth, the empress uttered not a sound of pain or distress and directed that her face be hidden from view — for, according to royal custom, the birth-chamber was thronged with bystanders. This stoical woman had charge of her son's upbringing until her death in 1539, and it is not surprising therefore that iron self-control also marked Philip's many-sided character.

As his father's sole heir, Philip grew up with an understanding of his own extreme importance. All his life he moved with the assurance of one convinced that he had a divine mandate to rule. But he was not overbearing. He knew how quickly disaster could overtake even great kings and dynasties — and if he needed to be reminded, occasional visits to his grandmother, the mad Juana, locked in her castle at Tordesillas, were enough to make the most exuberant prince sober and thoughtful. His father was away from Spain for long periods at a time, leaving Philip to grow up under the guidance of the Empress Isabella and a series of carefully chosen tutors. The young prince was said to be extraordinarily intelligent; he excelled at mathematics, studied architecture with a special interest, and had a taste for art, music, and poetry. He did not care for languages, and later said he wished he had studied them with greater care. He was taught Latin and Spanish as a matter of course, and French and German

against the day when he should visit his future territories in the north.

Charles oversaw his son's education from a distance and when the boy was fourteen the emperor began a concerted program for educating him in practical kingcraft. At this early age Philip was sent to lead Spanish troops against the French, who were attempting to take the Spanish-held border city of Perpignan. Seasoned generals conducted the military operations, of course, but the very presence of the royal heir in his armor and plumed helmet inspired the troops — and apparently discouraged the enemy. The French retired without a battle, and Philip made a triumphal entry into Perpignan.

Charles's next act was to appoint his son Regent of Spain, while he himself devoted all his attention to warring with France. No doubt remembering the *comunero* rebellion, he advised Philip to beware of the nobility, especially in connection with internal affairs. Nobles, he said, could be used but never fully trusted. The most reliable counselors, he believed, were members of the clergy, but in the end the only friend for a king was God. "On the whole I have much reason to be satisfied with your behavior," Charles wrote to his son, "but I would have you perfect. And, to speak frankly, whatever other persons may tell you, you have some things to mend yet."

At the age of sixteen this serious, reserved, conservative boy was married to his first cousin Maria of Portugal, an attractive girl about Philip's own age. It might be pointed out that marriage between cousins was an old custom among royalty, but in Spain the practice was more common than in other countries.

A limestone portrait medallion (left) of the type used to decorate archways and window frames in sixteenth-century Spain shows Charles V's son and heir, Philip, at age twelve. A mere four years later the prince was wed to his cousin Maria of Portugal — and little more than a decade after that the battle-weary and prematurely aged emperor abdicated in Philip's favor. As a sign of respect for his father, Philip II used Charles's campaign stool (below) as his throne at the Escorial.

In addition, three Spanish kings married their nieces, which no other European rulers were to do. In Philip's immediate ancestry, Ferdinand and Isabella were first cousins, as were Charles V and Isabella of Portugal. Of Philip's four wives, two were his first cousins, and the last was his niece.

Prince Philip was popular in Spain and so was his marriage with the Portuguese infanta. It was considered a wise political alliance, and besides, the wedding gave an excuse for riotous festivities that were a welcome diversion in the poverty-stricken country. Unfortunately, Princess Maria died less than two years later, in July of 1545, a few days after giving birth to a son, Don Carlos, who was to cause his father much grief. Philip remained a widower for nearly ten years.

According to a Venetian delegate to the Spanish court, Philip had a weakness for women, "with whom he amuses himself to an astonishing extent." In later years, Philip's enemies made him out to be a roué. William of Orange wrote that he was grossly licentious and that, moreover, he had been secretly married at the time he wed Maria of Portugal. Where William of Orange got his information is not recorded, however, and only two mistresses of the king are known by name. In any event, Philip seems to have been an attentive husband to each of his four wives, and contemporary observers were unanimous in insisting that all four adored him.

In appearance, Philip resembled his father. He was small in stature, had light brown hair, blue eyes, and the unattractive Habsburg jaw. In spite of his fairness he had a Spanish look. His expression was habitually grave, his eyes hooded. No one could have said what he

Some years before Charles V's formal abdication, his imposing profile and authoritative stance were captured by an unknown artist who chose to depict the emperor (far right) and his family in full court regalia. Philip, who stands to the left of his father, gazes upon his portly mother, Empress Isabella, and his ill-fated first wife, Maria of Portugal. Brilliantly colored royal escutcheons lie at the feet of Spain's first Habsburg rulers.

was thinking; whether he was giving orders for an execution or for a fiesta, his countenance was the same. As a young man his wardrobe was as splendid as that of any prince in Europe, but in later life he ordinarily dressed in somber black velvet or brocade with a white ruff and a black velvet hat, sometimes trimmed with plumes. It is said that he ordered new costumes often and gave the old ones to members of his household.

Philip was a widower of twenty-one when Charles V decided that his heir should make a grand tour of the empire. The young prince had never been out of Spain, and the Castilians protested his departure, fearing lest they acquire an absentee prince as well as an absentee king. After visiting various parts of Aragon, Philip set sail for Italy, escorted by a large fleet under the command of the great Genoese admiral Andrea Doria. Genoa and Milan, recent additions to his father's empire, were on Philip's itinerary, but he did not call on the pope, who would almost certainly have handed him a long list of complaints.

From Milan Philip traveled through the Tirol and several German states, joining his father at Brussels in the spring of 1549. The Flemings and Burgundians liked him no better than the Spanish had liked Charles some thirty years earlier. Philip spoke little French and no Flemish, and he was a fish out of water in the noisy, hard-drinking court. He did not like feasting all night, as his father did, and he was horrified to observe first-hand how deeply entrenched the Reformation was in the north. Charles had been unable to extirpate this heresy, partly because he was so preoccupied with other matters and partly because political expediency called for moving quietly. Young Philip was deeply respect-

ful of his august father and never challenged his will. Nevertheless, he was sincerely pious and he found particularly difficult those lessons in statesmanship that called for sitting down to dinner with Protestants and making war on the pope.

Had he been less power-hungry, Charles would have realized that the King of Spain could never succeed in controlling the Low Countries, and that the trouble they caused prevented him from effectively ruling the rest of his possessions. Blind to the obvious lack of rapport between Philip and the people of the Low Countries, he never ceased to plot how best to bind these countries to his dynasty.

In 1554 Charles hit upon the plan of marrying Philip to the new Queen of England, Mary, daughter of Henry VIII and Catherine of Aragon. Mary was a Roman Catholic and a Hispanophile, and she took kindly to the idea. Charles proposed to make their heir, should they have one, king of the Low Countries as well as of England; Spain and its possessions were to go to Philip's son by his first marriage, Don Carlos. But Charles was overly optimistic. The bride was a maiden of thirty-eight and in poor health. The only result of her union with Philip was a false pregnancy that proved to be nothing more than a combination of edema and hysteria. She died four years later, in 1558.

Meanwhile, Charles had decided to abdicate — a step that had not been taken by an important ruler since Roman times — and he began by ceding control of the Low Countries to Philip in a ceremony at Brussels in October of 1555. The following year he turned over to Philip the crown of Spain, and not long after that the German electoral princes accepted Charles's abdication as Holy Roman Emperor in favor of his younger brother, Ferdinand.

A lifetime of hard work and lusty recreation had made Charles old and tired before his time. Although only fifty-five, he already suffered from the ailments of an old man — arteriosclerosis, toothlessness, and senility. In his prime, however, Charles had been a formidable opponent and an aggressive imperialist — in the words of the seventeenth-century Spanish dramatist Pedro Calderón de la Barca, a "divine eagle who, in its tireless, inimitable flight holds the world under its wings." His vast colonial empire, aside from his Iberian possessions, had stretched from the Netherlands in the north, through central Europe (Luxembourg, Lorraine, Franche-Comté, Germany, and Austria), to parts of Italy, North Africa, and across the Atlantic to the rich, boundless territories of the New World. Ultimately, however, it had proved too much, both for his energies and his resources. By 1556, the Turks were dogging his heels along the North African coast; and his Spanish and Italian possessions were bled dry by expensive and relentless imperialist campaigns.

Yet Charles's reign, if fraught with disappointments, was not a total failure. If he taxed his Spanish kingdoms — particularly Castile — heavily, he also provided expanded markets for their goods and spurred industry to new heights. His regime saw the flowering of the golden age of Spanish art, literature, and humanism; and he gave Spain an efficient system of government. In the New World, he greatly extended the Spanish domains and firmly established a hold on South America. And finally, despite some setbacks, he was able to leave his son the bulk of his empire intact, secure in the conviction that Philip, if not as adventurous as he, would shepherd it with prudence.

In 1556 Charles retired to Yuste, a remote spot in the mountains of western Spain, and he spent the last two years of his life in a monastery of the strict Hieronymite order. He went not as a monk but as a private individual — to find peace and, perhaps, to do penance for his intemperate past. On September 21, 1558, he died and was buried at the monastery, dressed in the rough habit of a monk. In his will he asked his son to prepare a fitting tomb where he might lie beside his empress, Isabella of Portugal.

For at least a year before his father's death Philip had been thinking of building a great monument to the glory of God, to the Spanish martyr Saint Lawrence, and to the royal dead of the Spanish Habsburgs. He had first conceived of such a building in August 1557, on the occasion of a decisive Spanish victory against the French at the battle of Saint-Quentin. It was a highly important coup, one that Charles and Philip had been trying to bring about for a number of years. The events that precipitated that decisive clash were these: Pope Paul IV, elected in 1555, was virulently anti-Spanish and wanted Spain out of Italy. The French king, Henry II, volunteered to drive them out, and when someone suggested to the pope that the French might become an equal nuisance, he replied, "The French may easily be dislodged hereafter; but the Spaniards are like dog-grass, sure to strike root wherever it is cast." One reason the Spaniards were like dog-grass was that they had an excellent army with effective commanders: they beat the French in a confrontation near the borders of the kingdom of Naples. Philip then pre-

pared to strike at France from the Spanish Netherlands, to force the French into a war on two fronts.

Philip was no soldier. He disliked having to make up his mind in a hurry — an essential requirement on the battlefield. But he knew how to pick efficient generals, and on the northern borders of France he had placed the Duke of Savoy at the head of some 50,000 English, German, Burgundian, and Spanish troops. None of the French border fortresses were well manned, and Savoy directed his attack at one of the feeblest, Saint-Quentin. The French commander realized that his case was hopeless unless he could bring in reinforcements, which he thought he could do under cover of battle. Accordingly, at dawn on August 10, he struck at the Spanish, hoping to catch them unprepared. The result was an all-day battle that left thousands of French dead, wounded, or captive. The troops of Spain suffered considerable losses but they won the day, and when the news was brought to Philip, who was at Cambrai, some twenty-five miles away, he fell to his knees and thanked Saint Lawrence, whose feast-day falls on August 10. At that moment, he made a solemn vow to build the saint the greatest church in Spain.

When old Emperor Charles, in his monastery at Yuste, received news of the battle, he grumbled that Philip should have followed up his advantage and taken Paris. But it was not for nothing that Philip came to be known as the Prudent King. He remembered that a similar effort by his father had ended in failure, and he had, after all, accomplished his objective, which was to force Henry II to the peace table. Two years later, in April 1559, a peace was concluded at Cateau-Cambrésis with advantageous terms for

Spain. One proviso called for Philip's third marriage, this time with Henry's daughter, Elizabeth of Valois (or Isabella, as she is known in Spanish history), a pretty girl of fourteen. At the celebrations in honor of the proxy marriage in Paris, the bride's father insisted on taking part in a tournament and was mortally wounded by a lance splinter, thus subjecting France to the rule of several weak kings and a half century of bitter and inconclusive strife between Catholics and Huguenots.

A few months before the marriage, Philip returned to Spain. He was never to leave Iberia again. Almost at the end of an otherwise swift and pleasant voyage, the royal fleet encountered a severe storm off the coast of Galicia. Several ships were wrecked, and Philip must have experienced some alarming moments before his flagship reached safe harbor. The royal party had been at sea on Saint Lawrence's Day and one of Philip's earliest biographers attributed the king's safe home-coming to the saint's continuing goodwill toward him.

Two years had elapsed since the day Philip made his original vow to Saint Lawrence, and in the interim Charles V had died, bequeathing his son the task of constructing a royal mausoleum to house the emperor's remains. Spurred by this double obligation — one spiritual, one temporal — Philip began to formulate his great plan for a church and family tomb, to which he would adjoin a Hieronymite monastery and a palace for the royal family and court. He wanted to represent in architecture both his exalted kingliness and strength upon earth and his piety and humility before God. But perhaps above all he longed for a very personal retreat for himself.

II

The Vow Fulfilled

When Philip returned to Spain in 1559, one of his first acts was to give Spain the capital it had never had. He selected Madrid, at that time a small, rather ramshackle town, far less attractive than many other Spanish cities. But it was central, and to quote one of Philip's chroniclers, it gave "a heart to the great body of the Kingdom. . . ." With this resolution accomplished, that chronicler continues, Philip "turned to the next task, to find the best possible site for the great project that he carried in his breast."

Philip sought a solitary and peaceful place, yet one not too remote from his new capital. He roamed the wild Guadarrama Mountains that lie between Madrid and Segovia and considered a site occupied by a monastery of Hieronymites, the monkish order favored by his father. But after spending some time examining and considering this region, he decided that it was too rugged and inaccessible. Philip then named a council of architects, learned men, educators, and doctors to advise him, and after some debate he settled upon a southern slope of the Guadarramas about thirty miles north of Madrid. The chosen site was barren save for the remains of iron mines that had been worked out hundreds of years before; the tiny local hamlet of Escorial derived its name from the heaps of scoria, or slag, left by those early miners. The site was level enough to accommodate an enormous building, and there were both potable water and plenty of strong building stones — a pale granite flecked with pyrite — not far away. We are told by Fray José de Sigüenza, a Hieronymite monk who left a detailed record of the building of the Escorial, that the stone has within it "a luster and noble grandeur. . . . It is very uniform

in color and hardness, so that all the pieces weather equally." When completed, Sigüenza records, the building looked like "one piece, carved from one matrix."

Nearby were forests that would supply abundant firewood. These wooded areas teemed with deer, wild pig, rabbits, and other game, and the streams were alive with fish. Whenever plague decimated Spain, as it did regularly over the centuries, people sought this particular region as a refuge; the climate was comparatively temperate and, according to Sigüenza, even in the harshest winters the monastery's holy water did not freeze.

Philip was a very methodical man with a penchant for records, letters, and official documents. Having concluded that he had at last found the perfect site, he recorded his decision with characteristic formality:

In acknowledgment of the many and great blessings which it has pleased God to heap on us and continue to us daily, and inasmuch as He has been pleased to direct and guide our deeds and acts to his Holy service . . . considering likewise what the emperor and king, my lord and father, in a codicil which he lately made, committed to our care and charged us with, respecting his tomb, the spot and place where his body and that of the empress and queen, my lady and mother, should be placed; it being just and meet that their bodies should be most duly honoured with a befitting burial ground, and that for their souls be said continually masses, prayers, anniversaries, and because we have, besides, determined that whenever it may please God to take us away to Him, our body should rest in the same place and spot near theirs. . . . For all these reasons we found and erect the Monastery of San Lorenzo el Real, near the town of El

Escorial, in the diocese and archbishopric of Toledo, the which we dedicate in the name of the Blessed St. Lawrence, on account of the special devotion which, as we have said, we pray to this glorious saint, and in memory of the favor and victories which on his day we received from God. Moreover, we found it for the order of St. Jerome, on account of our special affection and respect for this order, and that which was also bestowed upon it by the emperor and king, my father.

The Hieronymites, followers of Saint Jerome, were one of the most severe and disciplined orders. Originally hermits, they had been ordered by a fourteenth-century pope to live in monastic communities. When they arrived in Spain at the beginning of the fifteenth century, they adopted the rule of Saint Augustine. With royal patronage they set up schools, hospitals, and hostels for pilgrims. Some Hieronymites, like their patron saint, were eminent scholars, and many were bold adventurers who accompanied the *conquistadores* to America and ventured into the uncharted wilderness to bring Christianity to the Indians.

Those who remained in monasteries lived in great seclusion, following prescribed rules for every minute detail of their lives. Sigüenza's observation about the holy water notwithstanding, it was bitterly cold in the foothills of the Guadarramas in the winter. The wind was damp and biting and the great drafty church was totally without heat — yet the monks began each day at midnight, when they gathered in the sanctuary for two to four hours of matins. After matins the monks slept until dawn, then rose again for mass and other services that lasted until the first meal of the day at eleven. The Hieronymites' food was simple — fish, meat once or twice a week, black bread, fruit. To our nutrition-oriented age such a diet sounds excellent, and it may well have been one reason for the great longevity of many of the brothers, but in comparison with the heavy diet of the Spanish court it was austere indeed. Afternoons at the monastery were spent in silent prayer, manual labor, and study, with a few minutes' free time for a quick siesta or a bit of conversation. Complin, the last liturgical rite of the day, was sung before supper, and the retiring bell rang soon after nightfall.

Among the more learned and distinguished Hieronymites was the aforementioned Fray José de Sigüenza, whose writings have been called "a kind of Escorial of [Spanish] classical literature, a model of sensitivity, sobriety, majesty, and clarity." Sigüenza's histories of the Escorial and of the Hieronymite order have not been translated into English, because they are of more interest to ecclesiastical historians than to ordinary readers. Indeed, three-fourths of his 1598 masterwork, *The Foundation of the Monastery of El Escorial*, is a painstaking description of church ceremonies and art works. The rest, however, is vivid, quaint, and full of human interest.

Fray José was born in the Castilian town of Sigüenza in 1544. At the age of twelve he presented himself at a Hieronymite monastery as a novice, but was told that he was too young. After some years as a student he decided to join an expedition that was setting out from Valencia to aid the Knights of Malta in their struggle against the Turks, but arrived in Valencia just in time to see the galleons of the expedition disappearing over the horizon. In 1565 he again presented himself to the Hieronymites, and this time was admitted.

Over the years Sigüenza became renowned for his learning and for his eloquence in the pulpit. For unrecorded reasons he had a brush with the Inquisition, but he received only a light sentence — several months of penance and sequestration. His abilities eventually brought him to the attention of Philip, who selected him in 1590 to catalogue and arrange the library of the Escorial and to oversee the final stages of its decoration. Sigüenza was made prior of the monastery sometime in the late 1590's, and died there in 1606. Philip praised the talented monk in the highest terms: "Those who come to see . . . this marvel of the world, that is the monastery, miss its principal wonder if they fail to see Fray José de Sigüenza; and deservedly his fame will outlast that of the building itself. . . ."

As Sigüenza later recorded, workmen began clearing the site for the Escorial in the spring of 1562, leaving trees all around it so that the peasants would have shelter for their flocks in winter and a place to keep watering troughs and take siestas in summer. That such matters were of genuine concern to the king is evident from Sigüenza's account. Before the first stone was laid, His Majesty had seen to it that a hospital was ready for sick or injured workmen. As the work crews grew more numerous, the number of beds increased from ten to more than seventy, and the patients reportedly were "so well cared for that many became well with no other medicine than comfort and cleanliness." For those who did not recover, the king also had special thought. The attendants, he wrote, "must display patience and love," and "when a patient is in his death agony, the bells should be rung so that he be prayed for in the village and the monastery, and die not like a beast." Philip

also established pensions for families of deceased workers and even instituted workmen's compensation; by royal decree one man whose badly burned leg had to be amputated received three hundred *reales*.

In the hamlet of Escorial, the house of the priest "often served as a palace for *El Rey* [the king] Don Felipe," as the other houses lacked windows and chimneys, and each had but one door "for light, smoke, beasts, and men." While the foundations were being dug, the king came often from Madrid, accompanied by a few high-ranking nobles, to "give heat to the work" by his presence. He heard mass in a tiny chapel, sitting on a three-legged stool made from a tree stump (which, "for decency's sake," the priests attending the monarch would cover with a worn French silk handkerchief). Fray Antonio de Villacastín, who served as acolyte, later wrote of his distress at finding that when the king and he both knelt in the miniscule chapel their feet nearly touched. He added that he had on occasion stealthily raised his eyes and had observed those of the king running with tears, "so great was his devotion and tenderness mixed with joy . . . thinking of the great plan that he had in his mind and the grandeur to which he proposed to raise that tiny holy place."

The workmen's hours were, for that day and age, remarkably reasonable: in the summertime they labored from six in the morning until eleven and from one in the afternoon until sunset, with a half-hour break at four o'clock; in winter they worked from sunrise to midday and from one until sunset. Sigüenza notes:

> The sainted king felt that these people were neither slaves nor pagans . . . like the thousands who worked on Solomon's temple, but Christians who make their

living by the sweat of their brows; he thought of them as his own brothers, not allowing the zealous foremen to force them. . . . For this reason I do not much admire the buildings of the Romans and other pagan and barbaric people, because they built them tyrannically, at the cost of miserable slave people, giving them no payment nor other satisfaction than beatings and death; and as the blood of innocents always cries out with unceasing voices to God for vengeance, it is no marvel that that prideful and tyrannical vanity perished so miserably, leaving behind scarcely its ashes.

The king followed the working operations at Escorial in exhausting detail. It was an empire in miniature, and perhaps more satisfying to its ruler than the real one, for it was all there before his eyes. The royal archives of Spain are swollen with Philip's meticulous records of the building of the Escorial: contracts with painters and sculptors, orders for lead or silver, plans for safeguarding valuables, even the appointment of chaplains for the laborers — all are there, signed in Philip's characteristic large, upright handwriting, "*Yo, El Rey* [I, the King]."

The first stone was laid in April 1563. Despite Philip's continual efforts to "give heat to the work," progress was slow. After ten years, the monastery and a small church within it were finished, but the main church was scarcely begun and the palace not yet livable. "Seeing that there were now enough monks to take care of the ceremonies with decent solemnity," Philip began the business of collecting the bodies of deceased members of the royal family from various parts of the country. First the body of Charles V was removed from its grave at Yuste and conveyed to the Escorial in an elaborate procession. Then the remains of several royal children who had died in infancy were disinterred, as were the corpses of four queens — Philip's mother, his third wife (who died in childbirth in 1568), and two of his sisters, the late queens of France and Hungary. When all the coffins were assembled at the monastery, they were placed in front of the church on a thirty-three-foot-high catafalque covered with brocade and black velvet and protected by a brocade canopy. After a long religious service, each was taken into the church for a day of masses and other obsequies, after which the royal coffins were placed in a crypt to await final burial in the as yet unbuilt pantheon.

While these rites were in progress, a great storm arose that ripped the rich black draperies off the coffins and scattered bits and pieces of velvet far away over pastures and forest. "People who lived here said they had never known such a wind," reports Sigüenza, who then offers his own explanation of the phenomenon:

Because these things tormented the bad angels and so many pious and holy acts made them angry and envious, everything having gone off on time and in an orderly manner with nothing going wrong and everyone being content, the princes of Darkness began to stir up the weather and to let loose a wind so fierce and furious that it caused wonder and terror. It seemed that the doors of hell had been opened in order to tear down the stones of this house; since that was not possible, the furious rage was turned on the dais in front of the door.

Despite this interruption, the ceremonies continued. The king, ever obsessed with clerical detail, directed that a parchment be placed inside each coffin giving the name, birthday, and death date of the deceased, and the date when the body was moved.

By 1575 Philip had already changed the original architectural plans to provide for a monastery twice as big as the one he had first envisioned. In that year he decided to change the plan of the church as well, putting aside the Latin-cross floor plan devised by Juan Bautista de Toledo, the original architect of the building, and substituting a Greek cross. During this same period Fray Antonio de Villacastín, the monk who had been so concerned about his feet touching those of the king at mass, was advanced to the position of Chief Overseer of Workmen. Sigüenza tells us that Fray Antonio was "not a man for jokes and fiestas," but when the cornerstone of the church was laid, he decreed a celebration. All the workmen, who then numbered nearly a thousand, paraded with their tools, which they carried like spears. Oxcarts followed, one carrying a workman dressed as Saint Peter with a key in his hand. Another workman, playing the part of Saint Lawrence, carried a grid, the symbol of the saint's martyrdom, and three women represented the three Marys. At the end of the parade came a young heifer, leaping and plunging about fiercely but harmlessly. Afterward there was dancing and *paseos*, the old Spanish custom of strolling about and greeting one's neighbors. "This fiesta," says Sigüenza, "was very amusing and caused many to repent, and even more so because it was the invention of such a holy monk who was so inimical to that sort of thing."

Not long thereafter, the monastery received a visit from the king's illegitimate brother, Don Juan of

Austria, whose recent victory over the Ottoman Turks
at Lepanto had made him the hero of the day. At this
juncture, the Devil, "who had caused no storms since
the reburial of the royal corpses, having been saving
up for this moment, caused a tremendous one . . . so
great a desire had he to discredit this site whenever
someone important came." Undismayed, Don Juan
toured the premises, paid homage to the relics, and
visited two old priors whose great age confined them
to bed. The monks, who had known Don Juan as a
child at Yuste — before he had been officially recognized as the son of Charles V — said that he acted as
simply and unpretentiously as he had before.

The great expense of the Escorial caused much murmuring in the kingdom, and it weighed on the king's
mind. He was therefore overjoyed when, in 1576, his
chief architect, Juan de Herrera, devised a new method
of working the stone at the quarries and of transport-
ing each block directly to its place in the wall, thus
eliminating the need for loading and unloading twice,
and saving a great deal of money and time. The chief
overseer, Villacastín, was suspicious of an untried
method and complained to Philip. Herrera explained
that the Greeks and Romans had built in this manner,
"but that this fact had been forgotten or perhaps never
known in Spain." Villacastín pointed out a lack of
facilities for the stoneworkers at the quarries, where-
upon the king signed "Yo, El Rey" to an order for
umbrellas and canvases to give protection from the
weather. He also authorized the construction of taverns
to provide after-hours refreshment. "The work," notes
Sigüenza, "which would have gone on for more than
twenty years was accomplished in less than six, in all

Porte na parte que pro mene dane 645 pies

the perfection that we now see and enjoy." Within a year the church was thirty feet high, the height of the floor of the choir and the upper cloister. Sculptures, paintings, and other embellishments for Philip's edifice were ordered in quantity from the hands of the foremost artists of Spain and Italy, but their delivery took many months, prompting the Duke of Alba to remark to His Majesty, "It takes longer to make the adornments for this building than to make the building itself."

Sigüenza detected the hand of God and of various saints assisting the great project at every turn:

> On the day of Saint Basil, that great pillar of the Church, they began to construct the bases of the four columns and the strong pilasters that sustain the whole weight of the church. I mention this because it was not planned purposely; the building went very fast and both the master builders and the unskilled laborers did their jobs without thinking what day it was, and Our Lord disposed fate so that what for men was chance or coincidence was ordered on days designated by Providence.

The good friar was more disposed to believe in good omens than in bad, and he refused to credit a story, prevalent among the workers one summer, that the Devil was wandering the passages of the Escorial in the guise of a large black dog, howling and dragging chains. The rumor persisted, and one night a number of witnesses reported such a dog running through the unfinished church to the very window of the king's apartment beside the high altar. The prior went out and seized the dog by the collar, took him into the cloister and hanged him, leaving the body for all to see, and thus putting an end to the story.

Sigüenza paints a delightful picture of the work-in-progress:

> I cannot decide whether it is more wonderful or more joyous to have seen the building when it was being built or now, when we behold it finished and perfect. Such noise and such a commotion! Such a variety of people with various voices; such a profusion of arts, offices, and tasks all going forward at once and with extraordinary diligence. And although it seemed a mass of confusion, in truth it was admirably planned and concerted, and caused amazement and wonder to newcomers. . . . In the church alone there were twenty two-wheeled cranes, some tall, some low . . . and above them scaffolds and platforms that reached to the sky. Those below called to those above; those in the middle now to one and now to the other. In the daytime, at night, in the afternoon, in the morning, one heard nothing but, "Hoist!" "Let go!" "Turn!" "Turn back!" "Draw!" "Stop!" "Look out!" Everyone shouted and the noise increased frightfully. . . . They seemed to be working not only to earn a living, as in other work, but to finish and perfect that which they had to do in an amiable strife and dispute, each wanting to be first but also to help the others. Besides the number of cranes in the church and its towers, there were others in various parts: in the apartments of the palace, in the royal house, and that of the ladies and *caballeros* [nobles], two more; in the main entrance, four or even six; in the hospital corridor, another; in the school, I don't know how many more; and to all were provided the necessary materials punctually and in abundance . . . carts, stones, lime, water, and wood.

An army of carpenters worked on doors, windows, and

such furniture as cupboards and chairs; there were masons, and people who worked with lime, stucco, plaster, bricks, tiles, and other building materials — "enough for an entire city." They were joined by numbers of embroiderers, who made vestments and hangings for the church; bell-makers and organ-makers; and people who made ropes, baskets, hawsers, cables, and other such necessities — "all these things' being made here at the foot of the building." The fields all around resounded with the sound of hammers, and besides workshops and smithies there were taverns "where people recovered their strength with wine." There were waterwheels where the hardest jasper and marble could be cut with emery and saws. And there were oxcarts, each carrying huge pieces of stone and each drawn by at least seven pairs of oxen, and sometimes by twelve, twenty, and even forty pairs. Everything was done at once: as soon as walls were in place, the carpenter came with his ready-made windows and doors; then came the smith with his bolts and rivets, and at the same time the roofers with their tiles and slates; then the painters and the locksmiths; and then, depending on the room, the artisans who installed the marble, jasper, colored tile, or brick flooring.

"There was scarcely a corner of the vast empire that did not send its most precious materials or wares to glorify the king's great palace," notes Sigüenza. Jasper was worked in the quarries near Burgos; bronzes for the church came from Zaragoza; white marble from the mountains of Extremadura; pine from Cuenca; balsam from Segovia; and silver lamps, chandeliers, censers, and crucibles from Toledo. Florence and Milan sent sculptures in bronze; Flanders sent bronze candelabras. And while work went forward on the building itself, the gardens, fountains, vineyards, orchards, and winepresses were also in the making, "all with the inspiration of the king, whose very presence gave life, being, and increase."

The year 1577 was greeted by astrologers with grave concern, and they begged Philip to beware in particular of the moment of eleven sevens that would occur — the twenty-first day (three sevens) of July (seventh month), in the seventh day of the moon, with the sun in the seventh grade of the sign of Leo, and so on. The king apparently placed little faith in astrology, for he commanded that all the bad predictions for the year 1577 be printed so that at the end of the year all could see that the astrologers had been wrong.

A number of unfortunate things did happen in 1577, none of them predicted. Sigüenza points out that no more calamities occurred than in most years, and he puts the blame on the Devil, not the stars:

> As the Enemy saw how much he was losing by this building . . . he tried in a thousand ways to delay its progress . . . sometimes with storms that broke out at the most inopportune moments, other times by disturbing the people of the towns and cities and making them believe that all the treasure of the kingdom was being wasted here; other times, by pretending that the King had changed his mind and was about to give the monastery to another Order . . . but the strength of our Prince was always greater than the effort, industry, and will of the Enemy.

So, in the year 1577, the Devil tried something new: he sparked a mutiny among the workmen in the quarry. The mayor of the town of Escorial had taken some of the workers into custody on some minor charge or another, and more to frighten them than to hurt them, proposed to have them whipped. The mutineers, who were Basques from the mountainous province of Vizcaya, surrounded the jail and threatened to kill the mayor. The next day work stopped in the quarries and the work bell was rung as a call to arms. With drum and banner the proud Basques thronged to the jail. The mayor opened the cells and released the prisoners, quelling the anger of the workers as easily as it had been aroused. They put down their arms willingly, and when the king arrived at the Escorial a few days later Fray Antonio de Villascastín intervened on the workers' behalf, saying that they had sinned no more than certain members of the lesser nobility — and fools. According to Sigüenza, "His Majesty laughed and answered kindly, showing in his great wisdom that he understood the truth of what the friar said. He did, however, send to the galleys those who had raised the banner and rung the bell, a punishment well deserved."

On a summer Sunday, the eve of Saint Magdalene, another terrible storm lashed the Escorial with a series of lightning bolts. One hit the sacristy, destroying several canvases and holy vessels; another damaged the church spire; and the strongest of the three struck the bell tower, knocking down several stones in the room inhabited by the bell-keeper, and setting fire to the highest belfry. The wood was dry and burned quickly, and the belfry was soon enveloped in flames. The bell-keeper did manage to ring the bells eleven times, but by the twelfth they had dissolved into ingots of bronze.

At the moment when the first bolt struck, Philip was preparing for bed. One of the guards came in to report

the incident, and the king asked serenely if any bystanders had been killed. "Learning that the answer was no, he thanked the Lord, being a God-fearing and pious prince who would be impious or insensate not to fear the divine wrath." Leaving his rooms accompanied by the Duke of Alba and other gentlemen, the king went to the hospital below the spire, which was then burning as bright as noonday. The duke, a faithful minister even though he was suffering from gout, climbed to the highest tower and supervised the fire fighters, a group comprised of workmen and servants. Some removed the burning beams as they fell; others fetched wet cloths, which they draped over the windows and doors to keep the fire from spreading; still others formed a human chain from a spring to the top of the tower and passed from hand to hand "a perpetual canal of water." The bronze ball and the cross that surmounted the spire melted and toppled to the ground — fortunately on the garden side, where they did little damage.

The heroes of the fire were two soldiers who had escaped from Turkish captivity in Constantinople and had come to the Escorial to ask the king for assistance. Before Philip's very eyes they threw burning beams from the windows of the tower into the cloister, and some of these "were so heavy that they would have been difficult to lift even stone-cold." The king granted the soldiers the rewards they asked for and more.

The monks, contributing in their own way to the fire-fighting effort, took a bit of the True Cross from the relic collection to give strength to the toiling men. Exhibiting the arm of Saint Lawrence, with which they hoped to ward off the Devil, the monks knelt, recited litanies, and gave food and drink to the fire fighters.

The bell-keeper who had sounded the first alarm by ringing the bells and shouting, "Fire! Fire in the bell tower!" fell a victim to smoke-poisoning, and though he rallied for a time, he died two or three years later.

The fateful year 1577 concluded with the appearance of a comet, which caused much foreboding. As Sigüenza notes, "it was later said . . . it threatened Portugal and that its tail and hair extended into Spain."

On June 23, 1582, the church was finished, with the cross on the spire of the dome being placed in position at exactly six in the evening. The cross, which was made of iron and weighed nearly a ton, stood thirty-one feet high and had eight-foot arms. The moment was marked by a solemn procession and Te Deums, followed by dancing and other festivities.

In November of 1584, the Escorial received some highly unusual visitors: "four Japanese gentlemen [who] were about fifteen or sixteen years old." Converted to Christianity by Spanish missionaries, they were on their way to see the pope. Their voyage from Nagasaki to Lisbon by way of Ecuador and around the horn had taken thirty months. The king sent them in carriages from Madrid to the Escorial, where the prior gave them a red-carpet tour. Later they wrote the king a thank-you letter that is still preserved in the library: "We are full of great wonder and are happy to have seen such a magnificent thing, such as we never saw before nor dreamed of seeing. All the labors and dangers of the three-year journey were worth it, having brought us to see such a marvelous thing."

The last stone in the vast complex — a cornice stone in the church portico that is still pointed out by guides today — was laid in September 1584. Fray Antonio de

During his seventeen-year tenure as head architect,
Herrera executed hundreds of working sketches of
the unfinished Escorial, among them a detailed
cross-section of the basilica (below). Many, such as
the elevation at right, bear the architect's bold
signature. Herrera's concern over each aspect of the
project is evidenced in the sketch at right center,
which shows the inner workings of the mill, whose
fluted drive-shaft was turned by water funneling in
from outside. Philip took an equally zealous
interest in the project, and it was he who ordered
that the finials capping the first story of the
basilica's façade (lower right) be replaced
by white marble statues of six biblical kings.

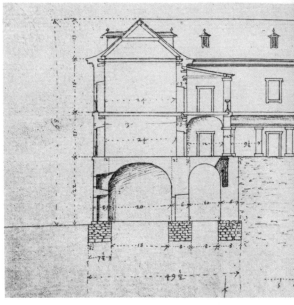

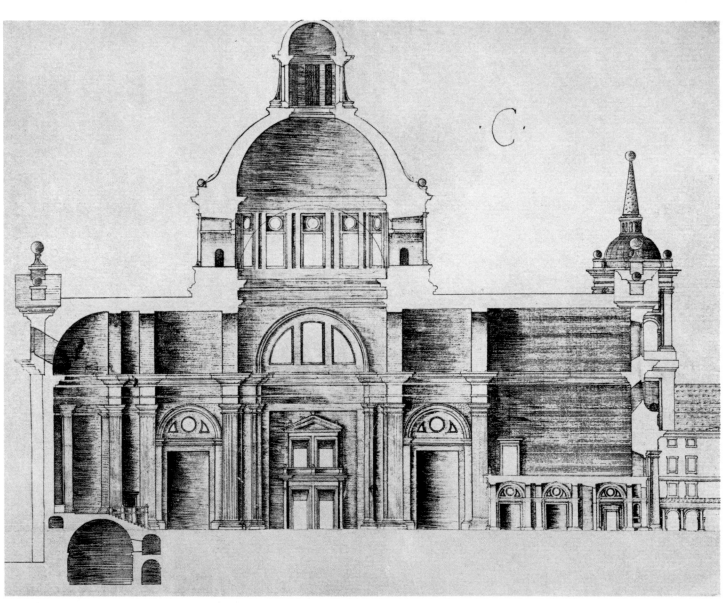

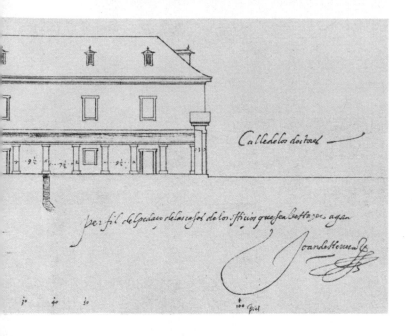

Calle de los doctores

perfil del pedaco de las casas de los officios que se an de hazer agora

Joan de Herrera

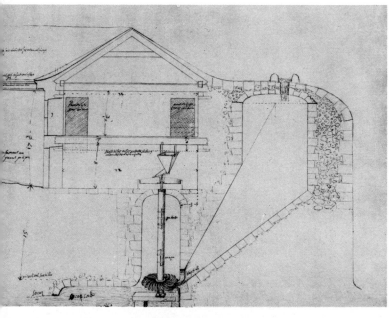

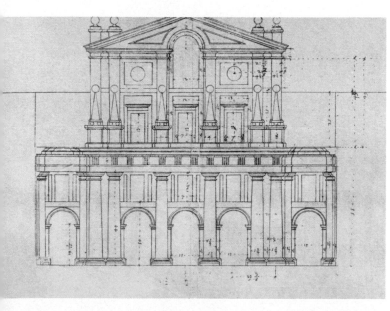

Villacastín had been at the Escorial during the laying of the cornerstone twenty-one years before, but he had refused to attend those ceremonies, apparently feeling that if he did not see the first stone laid he would see the last; and this he did.

Philip and his children came to the dedication ceremonies, which lasted for days and were attended by large crowds from Madrid, Segovia, Avila, and even from as far away as Toledo. Relics were shown from the windows of the choir, where the king sat with his son, the future Philip III. Here he often sat thereafter, coming in unnoticed while the monks sang matins or vespers. Later that year there were new burial ceremonies, as the royal dead were transferred from a chapel within the monastery to a crypt below the high altar of the new church. In the following century, when the Pantheon of the Kings was finished, they would be moved once more.

Now that the building was completed, the king was often in residence. Nearly every year he spent Holy Week with the monks, washing the feet of twelve old paupers on Maundy Thursday and serving them dinner. The day after Easter 1589, Philip attended the baptism of a Moroccan Jew, a leading citizen of Fez. At His Majesty's direction, Prince Philip and the Infanta Isabella Clara Eugenia served as godparents. Before departing, Philip invariably went on a tour of the entire building and gave directions for further work; for although the actual construction was over, there was still much to be done in the way of embellishment. The Escorial, the king once said, was *"la dama de sus amores"* ("the lady of his heart").

The last great ceremony held during Philip's life-

time was the consecration of the church of San Lorenzo el Real on August 30, 1595. The ceremonies on this occasion outdid all previous ones, and Sigüenza describes them in exhaustive detail. A high point was the illumination of the entire Escorial with *luminarias,* earthenware lamps filled with burning oil and fitted with oiled paper shields to keep out the wind. The infanta's ladies made the wicks, and at nightfall on August 30 they were lit, "making one of the most joyous sights that could be imagined." Every window contained a *luminaria,* and there were so many on the ledges and moldings of the towers and dome, and in the garden, "that there seemed to be no interval between them. . . . It made a vision so beautiful in the midst of that somber building that it was like no earthly thing. . . . The illumination could be seen from Toledo and even from Ocaña [nearly a hundred miles away]. Philip came out of his apartments, carried in a chair because he was incapacitated by gout. He went to the high cloister of the monastery to enjoy the view and the fruit of his blessed invention."

Wanting to see the Escorial from near and from far, the king had himself carried into the village and up the mountain slope. Sigüenza adds that it was a miracle that nothing went wrong that night because the lights were in high and dangerous places, "and many of the workmen and other people were as full of wine as the lamps of oil. In the midst of so many candles, God held them in his hand, because a night of such happiness could not be mixed with sadness." Many of the lamps were still burning at dawn, mingling their light with the light of the clear morning "until the sun's rays grew strong and the lamps were finished."

III

Architects and Artists

Philip II was a perfectionist. He looked for perfection in everyone in his employ and, above all, he expected it of himself. Like all such people, he was continually disappointed, and although he was almost blindly obsessed with the Escorial, he must have known that it was not an unqualified success. In truth, the fact that Philip's ambitious undertaking turned out as well as it did was largely due to his singular good fortune in finding two architects who not only had sparks of genius but who were able to work patiently and uncomplainingly under such an exacting master.

The first of these loyal and dedicated men was Juan Bautista de Toledo, a Spaniard who had spent most of his career in Rome, where he had worked on the basilica of St. Peter's, and in Naples, where he had served the king's viceroy. In 1559, Philip sent for Juan Bautista, appointed him architect-royal, and revealed the staggering project that he had conceived. Exactly which ideas for the Escorial's design were Philip's and which were Juan Bautista's will never be known with certainty. The king probably had a clearer idea of what he wanted than the average architectural client, and he certainly had some knowledge of the practical aspects of building. Juan Bautista brought to the task a lifetime of experience as well as recent exposure to the Italian architectural renaissance.

The basic design of the Escorial resembles a gridiron; solid masses surrounding open spaces (see diagram, page 167). The handle of the gridiron is represented by a solid rectangular structure, the private apartments of the royal family. It has often been suggested that Philip and his architect intended to represent the gridiron upon which Saint Lawrence suffered

martyrdom; perhaps they did have such a scheme in mind, but a gridiron-shaped building was not a novel concept in 1559. In the previous century, a large hospital in Milan had been laid out with many inner courtyards, and there were other examples of this style in contemporary Spain. Moreover, since ancient times a gridiron plan had been used for palaces by the peoples of the Near and Middle East. The Alhambra, built by Arabs in the southern Spanish city of Granada, is one example. (The Escorial is also similar to the Alhambra in having a portico, a court, and a second portico, all leading toward the place of worship.) But the example that Philip was most anxious to follow was that of the Temple of Solomon. No reliable plan of it was available, but according to tradition it too was laid out around a number of inner courts. Believing Solomon's temple to have been inspired by God, Philip liked to think that his Escorial was either a reconstruction or a logical result of that long-lost edifice.

The Escorial has been called a complex of unities. The entrance court and the church of San Lorenzo el Real mark the central unity, with the monastery on the right side, the college and part of the palace on the left, the royal apartments at the back, and the royal tombs at the core, beneath the high altar. What makes this enormous complex unique in the history of architecture is the way in which it melds size, pretension, and costliness with astonishing austerity. It seems likely that Philip himself insisted that it should be austere, for the other buildings designed by Juan Bautista were considerably more ornate.

Juan Bautista had St. Peter's dome in mind when he designed San Lorenzo el Real, but where St. Peter's dome is a mass of Corinthian columns, San Lorenzo's uses simpler Doric ones, and the rest of the embellishments are in keeping. If St. Peter's speaks for the High Renaissance, San Lorenzo is an architectural statement of the Counter-Reformation. "For beauty it depends not on decoration but on order, proportion, and harmony," says the art historian Georg Weise. "The Escorial is lucid and logical — like the theology of the Council of Trent."

Juan Bautista had the distinguished Italian engineer Francesco Paciotto to advise him on technical matters, and he possessed a staff of young Spanish assistants as well. One who showed particular ability and a prodigious capacity for work was Juan de Herrera. Born in 1530 of a well-to-do family in Asturias, Herrera was a typical Renaissance man. He was adventurous, both in worldly and intellectual pursuits, and although he had little formal education, he was an avid learner. In 1547, when he was seventeen, young Herrera went to Valladolid to enter the service of Prince Philip.

At the time, going to court was a relatively new fashion in Spain. During the reign of Charles V, who introduced the practice, it became almost mandatory for young gentlemen and noblemen to leave their estates and become courtiers if they wanted to advance in life. When Prince Philip set forth on his tour of Italy and the north, Herrera was in his train. The young man's duties cannot have been arduous, for he found time to study mathematics and philosophy and to dream of becoming an architect. Upon returning to Spain in 1551, however, he went into the army — perhaps it seemed a quicker way to fame and honors. He served in Italy and Flanders, and in 1554 became a member of the emperor's guard. In this capacity he returned again to his native country and was stationed at Yuste until Charles's death in 1558.

By 1561 Juan de Herrera was back at Philip's court, copying the illustrations in a medieval book on astronomy for young Don Carlos, Philip's eldest son. His copy may now be seen in the library of the Escorial; it shows curious and recondite drawings of astrological subjects. It was this assignment that apparently brought Herrera to the attention of the king. Philip needed assistants for his chief architect, Juan Bautista, but feared that if he appointed well-established architects to subordinate positions there would be rivalry and ill-feeling. After a typically protracted consideration of the problem, the king eventually named Juan de Herrera as one of Juan Bautista's assistants.

Herrera had never designed and constructed a building, but Juan Bautista must have been greatly impressed with his ability, for from the first he treated the neophyte almost as a collaborator. He took Herrera to visit other royal buildings that were being renovated or enlarged, among them the Alcazar in Madrid and the palace at Aranjuez. When Juan Bautista presented a wooden scale model of the proposed Escorial to the king, Herrera was among the few persons present. And to Herrera went the assignment of composing and designing the inscription on the cornerstone, which was laid in April 1563. Juan Bautista became ill in 1567 but was able to continue his work by directing Herrera from his sickbed. That year, Philip raised Herrera's salary from 100 ducats a year to 250. Two months later, Juan Bautista died.

Again Philip pondered deeply and with painful in-

By midafternoon, deep shadows blanket the 210-foot-long Patio of the Kings (above), shattering the symmetry of the basilica's Doric façade and focusing attention on the gilt and marble statues that adorn its first story. In the 1591 engraving at upper right, the sunlit patio is plainly visible beyond the main gate of the Escorial.

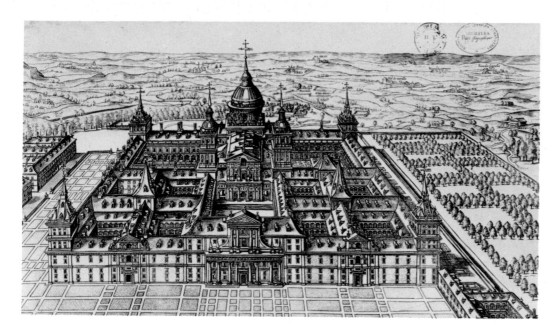

decision: whom should he place in this important position? At length he determined to give Herrera all Juan Bautista's former duties but not his title, and to accord him no further salary increase — this in order to avoid offending older, more experienced architects. From that time on, Herrera lived at the building site and was answerable only to His Majesty. Busy though he was, he found time to invent some ingenious nautical instruments, and Philip granted him ten years' exclusive right to manufacture them. Herrera also oversaw work on other royal buildings, and designed the façade of the Alcazar at Toledo. His brilliant innovations in the methods of cutting stone at the Escorial so accelerated the work that the grateful king raised Herrera's salary to eight hundred ducats a year.

In 1579 he was made royal custodian of the palace, a position that brought with it free access to the royal bedroom and the privilege of receiving orders directly from His Majesty. This was a rare privilege indeed, for such was the strict ceremony of the Spanish court that through fifteen years of almost daily contact with the king, Herrera had always had to communicate with him through a more august intermediary. It was Philip's habit to communicate with most of his numerous officials in writing — including those palace functionaries he dealt with on a daily basis.

It was awkward for a man of moderate means to live up to the style expected of an important courtier. The king helped Herrera by favoring him with revenues of certain copper and lead mines in Asturias and by allowing him the exclusive right to sell prints of the Escorial in Spain and in the Indies. Even so, and in spite of two advantageous marriages, Herrera found

court life prohibitively expensive, and when the last stone was laid at the Escorial he obtained Philip's permission to retire. He lived some thirteen years longer on the estates near Santander that he had acquired through his second wife, and he died there in January 1597. It is said that the king was deeply affected by the death of this brilliant and devoted servant, whose life-work had been so closely intertwined with the Spanish monarch's own.

"More than a description, El Escorial needs an itinerary," says a Spanish writer. Accordingly, let the reader imagine himself in front of the main entrance of the Escorial, ready for at least a day's pilgrimage through its vast precincts. The principal gate is set into the west façade, and its massive simplicity is a perfect introduction to what is to come. The overall design is Juan Bautista's, but architectural detectives have established the sources of some of its separate features. The lower story has alternating niches and windows in a manner favored by the renowned Italian architect Andrea Palladio, of whose work Juan Bautista must have been aware. The upper story is adorned with obelisks and Doric pillars and bears a distinct resemblance to a design for a church façade published in 1552 in Toledo. (A book containing this design is known to have been in Philip's library.) A granite and marble representation of Saint Lawrence holding a gilded bronze gridiron stands in a niche directly above the principal entrance.

Having passed through the west gate and then through a portico just inside it, one stands in the spacious Patio of the Kings, a long, stone-paved rectangle. The church of San Lorenzo el Real looms at the oppo-

From his special seat in the High Choir, Philip was able to see both the four-foot-high hymnals used in daily devotionals (left) and the distant altar with its triple-tiered retable. A close-up of the High Altar (right) reveals both the carefully draped altar itself and the domed tabernacle above it. That finely detailed jasper and bronze temple, which was designed by Herrera and executed by Jacome Trezzo over a seven-year period, has been called the most perfect of its kind ever made.

site end of the courtyard, which is named in honor of those biblical kings who were concerned with building the temple at Jerusalem — David, Jehoshaphat, Ezekiel, Solomon, Josiah, and Manasseh. Colossal granite statues of the six stand on the portico of the church, facing us. Juan Bautista's original plan had called for obelisks here, to relate the portico to the main gate, but Philip never hesitated to change the schemes of his architects. As one of the Venetian ambassadors to Philip's court observed, "His Majesty follows his taste rather than the rules of architecture."

All the statues — each weighing nearly a ton and each having a crown and insignia in gilded bronze — are the work of Juan Bautista Monegro, the only Spanish sculptor to make a major contribution to the Escorial. Born about 1545 and trained in Italy, Monegro spent most of his career in Toledo. In 1584, after the last stone of the Escorial had been laid, Philip commissioned these seven statues from him, perhaps to alleviate the exceeding severity of the courtyard. Other statues by Monegro adorn the main court within the monastery, the Court of the Evangelists.

As Fray Francisco de los Santos, seventeenth-century author of a book about the Escorial, remarked, "The prospect of this miracle of genius, skill, and architecture discourages any attempt to describe it." In Francisco de los Santos's time the vast stone courtyards and the cavernous interiors were thronged with people — servants, halberdiers, *caballeros* on prancing horses, beggars, great ladies, students of the college, and itinerant friars, to say nothing of the artists, craftsmen, and journeymen whose work there was never-ending. There were coaches arriving and departing, street peddlers

hawking food and wares, noblemen being carried in sedan chairs. There were barking dogs and braying pack-mules, and the smell of food, fires, and human sweat. All this has to be imagined by the present-day visitor, who sees nothing but gray granite walls and vast, empty courtyards.

We pass through the Patio of the Kings and enter the enormous and usually deserted church of San Lorenzo el Real. Rising above the center of the nave is Juan Bautista de Toledo's greatest achievement, a dome that is generally regarded as one of the most beautiful built during the Renaissance. It clearly owes much to Bramante's original plan for the dome of St. Peter's, but differs strikingly in being so little ornamented, both inside and out. Standing far beneath it, we look up to Doric half columns alternating with leaded windows of clear glass — and nothing else save the bare granite ribs of the dome itself.

The most elaborate part of the church is that surrounding the high altar, behind which a retable of red granite and jasper, adorned with life-size gilt-bronze statues and three tiers of paintings, rises to a height of eighty-six feet. By Philip's orders, the altar itself, which is made of jasper and precious marbles, is placed so that when mass is said the feet of the officiating priest are directly above the body of the Emperor Charles V, who lies buried in the crypt below. Juan de Herrera designed the splendid jasper and bronze House of the Sacrament — probably at the special behest of Philip, for whom the Sacrament was an object of particularly intense veneration.

If Philip could have had his way, he would have commissioned Michelangelo to design the Escorial and

Titian to decorate the three-tiered retable behind the high altar. But even kings cannot always command. Michelangelo was an octogenarian in frail health when the Escorial was begun, and he died in 1564, a year after the cornerstone was laid. Titian was also in his eighties by that time and gave advanced age as an excuse not to travel — although he continued to paint vigorously for many more years and lived to be ninety-nine. Veronese also declined the king's invitation, in spite of the prospect of excellent pay and working conditions. Thus Philip had to make do with lesser Italian artists recommended by his ambassadors. They came in large numbers: painters, sculptors, and craftsmen. One painter, Federigo Zuccaro, highly recommended by the king's ambassador in Rome, arrived with a retinue of five and was awarded a salary of two thousand ducats a year. Over a period of three years he painted part of the great retable, other altar pieces, and several frescoes in the principal cloister. According to Sigüenza, "He painted all that and very little of it pleased the king or anyone else."

When Philip came to see the finished paintings for the high altar, he conducted his review in silence, "for he never liked to hurt anyone." Finally, pausing at a Nativity scene, he asked the artist whether one of the shepherds was carrying eggs in a basket. Zuccaro replied in the affirmative. "Everyone present," Sigüenza records, "could see that it was an inappropriate thing for a shepherd, coming from his flocks at midnight and on the run at that, to be bringing all those eggs, unless he had been looking after chickens."

Not long thereafter, Philip gave Zuccaro permission to return to Italy. The munificent salary promised the Italian painter was paid in full, and the king observed, "It was not his fault, but the fault of those who sent him here." One tier of Zuccaro's retable paintings has survived, but most of his other efforts were destroyed.

The story of the eggs illustrates Philip's passion for logic, even in art. Only in religious matters could he accept the illogical. Miracles were one thing, but a shepherd running about at midnight with a basket of eggs under his arm — even in the presence of a miracle — was quite another. In fact, it was because of his insistence on the realistic and the logical that Philip was dissatisfied with the only painter of genius who ever had anything to do with the original decoration of the Escorial. That painter was El Greco.

Many of the facts about El Greco's life are obscure. It seems certain that his real name was Domenico Theotokopoulos and that he was born in Crete in 1548. He studied in Venice, where he was influenced by Titian, Tintoretto, and Bassano, and gained a reputation in Rome, where he became known as "the Greek." Later he went to live and work in Toledo, and there he came to Philip's attention through his painting *The Adoration of the Name of Jesus by Heaven, Earth, and Hell.* Some art historians believe that El Greco sent this painting to the king as an example of his work, hoping to get commissions at the Escorial. In a canvas thronged with indistinct, other-worldly figures, Philip stands out sharply. Unlike the others, who wear pastel robes, Philip is attired — as was his wont — all in black, with black gloves and a white ruff. His eyes are turned heavenward and he ignores everyone else. The denizens of Hell are behind him, where he will not have to look at them, for only Heaven is of interest to a man such as Philip. As the lonely and aloof site of the Escorial reflects the character of the man who built it, so too does this canvas, which depicts Philip physically and spiritually isolated in the midst of hundreds.

The king was apparently so impressed with the painting that he commissioned El Greco to work at the Escorial. Philip's favorite Spanish painter, the deaf-mute Domenico Navarrete, called El Mudo, died in 1579 leaving much work to be done. For the retable, Philip ordered El Greco to paint a *Martyrdom of Saint Maurice*. But when the work was finished it failed to please Philip, although he did include it in the art collection he was forming. The painting was too emotional and too unrealistic to suit a king who objected to shepherds carrying eggs. Furthermore, Philip thought that the actual martyrdom should be taking place in the foreground of the picture, not where El Greco had put it, in the middle distance. El Greco was dismissed and one of the ubiquitous Italians, Romulo Cincinato, was requested to paint a new *Martyrdom of Saint Maurice* for the retable. The stilted and lifeless work that he produced was never placed there, but consigned to an obscure chapel.

El Greco apparently bore the king no grudges, however, for in his masterpiece *The Burial of the Count of Orgaz* he painted his former employer among the ranks of the blessed. The Escorial collections include four other works by El Greco: *Saint Peter, Saint Eugene,* and two studies of Saint Francis. In the end, two of the three tiers of paintings for the high altar were executed by the Italian Pellegrino Tibaldi.

The gilded bronze statues that form part of the retable are the work of a Milanese sculptor, Leone Leoni,

and his son, Pompeo. The impressive, larger-than-life-size kneeling groups on the right and left of the high altar are by Pompeo alone. The figures on the right represent Charles V, his wife, the Empress Isabella, his daughter, Maria, and two of his sisters. On the left are Philip II and his fourth wife, Anna of Austria. Behind them are Philip's son, Don Carlos, and the monarch's first and third wives (his second, Queen Mary of England, was buried in Westminster Abbey, and has been omitted from the grouping).

Except in the cases of Philip and Queen Anna, the sculptors worked from contemporary portraits. The resulting figures look remarkably lifelike, yet at the same time uncanny — perpetually and silently kneeling, with every ringlet, every fold of lace and brocade, and every finger frozen in place. All wear expressions of supreme composure rather than religious fervor, for Spanish royalty was never to display emotion in public. Fray Sigüenza notes that on one particular Good Friday Philip wept as he worshiped before the cross, and knelt while kissing it most reverently — but this he would never have done except among the cloistered monks. Leone and Pompeo Leoni worked on the figures for the retable and high altar over a period of three years. The casting was done in Milan, and the final bill came to the equivalent of $100,000, a not unreasonable sum for a commission of such size and scope.

One of the chief treasures of the Escorial is to be found in a chapel of San Lorenzo el Real: a marble Christ on the Cross, made in Florence in 1562 by Benvenuto Cellini. In his autobiography, Cellini tells us that he carved it according to a vision that appeared to him when he was imprisoned in Rome in 1527:

It is not surprising that Philip, who was conservative in nature and self-effacing in manner, should have failed to appreciate the flamboyant style of the one genuinely talented painter to work at the Escorial under his aegis. Nor is it any surprise that the painter — who was born Domenico Theotokopoulos but known even in his own lifetime as El Greco — should have understood his patron almost perfectly. For El Greco was discerning where Philip was obtuse — as the large canvas at right clearly indicates. That work, titled The Adoration of the Name of Jesus but more commonly called The Dream of Philip II, is anchored by the black-clad, kneeling figure of the king (center foreground). Blissfully unaware of the inmates of Hell who cluster behind him — and equally oblivious to the supplicants in front of him and the swirling spectacle above him — Philip is lost in a spiritual world of his own. Indeed, it was the king's highly personal view of religion — and religious art — that led him to reject the first canvas he commissioned El Greco to paint. Philip wanted a conventional Martyrdom of Saint Maurice for the retable behind the High Altar; El Greco produced a darkling masterpiece (left) that relegated the saint to the middleground and flatteringly depicted his captors as elongated, ethereal, and benign. The concept was far too radical for Philip, who ordered the canvas consigned to his private collection instead. That collection includes El Greco's arresting study of Saint Francis (above), a classic example of the visual distortion and the chromatic control that hallmark El Greco's works.

> Although I have made several marble statues, I shall only mention one, from its being of a kind most difficult for art to render — that is, dead bodies; I speak of the image of Our Lord Crucified, for which I studied a great deal, working upon it with the diligence and love that so precious a simulacre deserves, and also because I knew myself to be the first who ever executed crucifixes in marble.

Cellini offered to present the sculpture, which is life-size, to his patroness, the Duchess of Tuscany. She declined to accept it as a gift, and the duke subsequently bought it. His son presented it to King Philip. The monks at San Lorenzo have seen fit to keep the naked loins of the statue draped with a white cloth.

The choir is about thirty feet above the main entrance to the church. Herrera designed the handsome choir stalls, which are carved of ebony, box, and other choice woods. When the craftsmen were ready to start making them, Philip was in Lisbon, engaged in the very taxing business of taking over the Portuguese throne. But such was his meticulous concern over everything that went into the Escorial that he had two sample stalls sent to him for approval before he would allow work to proceed. Herrera also designed a marble and bronze lectern for the choir, beautiful and ingenious as was nearly everything he put his hand to. Although it weighs several tons, it can be rotated with the touch of a finger.

A low door at one end of the choir gave the king access to one of the stalls, and there he frequently joined the monks at matins or vespers. Philip had his usual bad luck with the paintings he commissioned for this part of the church. Some of the wall frescoes are by

Observing that he was "the first who ever executed crucifixes in marble," Benvenuto Cellini sculpted the life-size statue of Christ at left for the Duke of Tuscany — whose son presented it to Philip. Hung from a cross of black Carrara marble, the figure dominates a niche in the south wall of the basilica. Also set into the south wall is the gilded bronze statue group below, one of two that the Leoni family of Milan created for Philip. This extraordinarily detailed and breathtakingly realistic grouping features Philip (lower right) and three of his four wives (from right to left: Anna, Isabella, and Maria of Portugal, whose son, Don Carlos, kneels behind her). Mary Tudor, whose remains are interred in Westminster Abbey, is conspicuously absent. The companion piece shows Emperor Charles V and the members of his family.

the undistinguished Romulo Cincinato, and the ceiling, by yet another Italian, Luca Cambiaso, has a second-rate depiction of *The Bliss of Heaven*. Included among the blissful are Fray Antonio de Villacastín — the monk who had been in charge of all the workmen during the building of the Escorial — and the artist himself. Fray Sigüenza, who disapproved of the immoral behavior of Luca and the other Italian artists, remarked dryly that this was as close to heaven as the artist was likely to get.

Most of the monastery is closed to the public, and we have to make do with photographs of some of the most beautiful parts of the Escorial. The Galeria de Convalecientes, so named because it is near the monastery hospital and affords a sheltered place for convalescent monks to sit or walk, is believed to be entirely the design of Juan Bautista de Toledo. Like the main gate, it is faintly reminiscent of the work of Palladio. The monastery side of the building faces south and presents the least forbidding of the four façades. It is softened by the presence of gardens and a large pool that reflects the long gray wall, the towers, and the sky.

All the gardens of the Escorial, both here and under the windows of the royal apartments, are now laid out in geometrical patterns with box hedges, but in Philip's time they were planted with brilliant flowers by a Hieronymite who was a specialist in landscape gardening. He was one of the first monks to arrive at the site of the new monastery (coming from Yuste, where he had been chief gardener), and he began planning the Escorial's gardens and orchards some time before the first stone was laid.

Spanish gardens of the period had a marked Moorish air, and the Moors, coming from the desert, had made much of gardens. For them the garden was a place of repose, full of the sound of running water and riotous with bright flowers and sweet scents. Medieval Spanish monks were often housed in former Moorish castles whose highly sensuous Moorish gardens were then taken over by chaste Christian brothers. But at the Escorial the Moorish tradition was modified by the Renaissance concept of a garden — open, spacious, and geometric. A traditional garden of either variety would have included tall trees — most likely cypresses, symbolizing immortality — but these were omitted for fear they would compete with the architecture. From the terraced gardens, stone steps led down to orchards. Sigüenza speaks of the landscaping:

> [There was an] infinite variety of plants, trees, and herbs, giving a great abundance of flowers. . . . Seen from the windows [the flower beds] have so many colors — white, blue, yellow, red, and multicolored — and are so well arranged, that they look like fine Turkish carpets brought from Cairo or Damascus. . . . [The gardens] are a comfort to the soul, they assist contemplation, and lift the thoughts to the beauty of Heaven.

Philip gave his personal attention to selecting the plants; he also established an apothecary's shop within the monastery where, besides preparing medicines, the brothers distilled perfume from roses, carnations, and lilies. The king's botanical bent is further evidenced by the fact that many surviving royal documents have to do with reforestation, water systems, ponds, and the collecting of new plant species. From Lisbon, where he was beset by the gravest political questions and

Enclosed by the graceful colonnade of the Cloisters, the Court of the Evangelists (left) provides a secluded haven for the monks who still maintain the sprawling edifice. An octagonal central shrine, lined with jasper and capped with a marble cupola, shields the statues of Matthew, Mark, Luke, and John that give the courtyard its name. The grand staircase (right), whose broad steps were cut from single slabs of granite, has been frequently copied. The stairwell itself is copiously decorated with frescoes depicting scenes from the life of Christ.

where he had just become a widower for the fourth time, Philip found time to write to one of his secretaries with a specific botanical query: "Ask Enrique, my tailor, the name of the tree that grows by his house, and let me know what it is. . . ."

In the great cloister of the monastery, known as the Court of the Evangelists, there was also a delightful flower garden. It is important to remember these vanished flowers, for Philip and his architects fully intended that they should be there to provide a softening contrast to the austere geometry of the building. The Court of the Evangelists has been called "beyond question the finest architectural work to be seen and admired in the Escorial." It was designed by Juan Bautista de Toledo and it plainly reflects the experience he garnered during his long years in Rome.

The grand staircase — also within the cloistered precincts of the monastery and not part of the regular sight-seeing agenda — was designed by one of Juan Bautista's assistants, an Italian known as the Bergamesco, and is the earliest known example of a style called the Imperial Staircase. It is believed to have been based on sketches by Leonardo da Vinci, and according to Fray Sigüenza it "is one of the most successful and beautiful things in El Escorial." One broad flight of stairs ascends to a landing, and from that point two flights continue upward at an angle of 180 degrees to the first. This very grand and spacious design was copied widely wherever special magnificence was in order. It is typical of Philip's extraordinary nature that he should place such a sumptuous staircase where it was regularly used by humble monks rather than by royalty and nobility.

A room of the monastery that was formerly the prior's cell has been arranged as a museum for the display of sixteenth-century vestments and small objects of art. The former were made at a needlework factory set up by order of the king in a house near the Escorial. Hieronymite monks were in charge of the factory, which for many years turned out some of the most elaborate and costly vestments and other priestly accouterments ever seen. Most striking, perhaps, are the funeral vestments made under Philip's aegis for his own obsequies: the chasuble itself is black velvet, heavily embroidered with silver thread in an overall design of skulls and crossbones.

When the library of San Lorenzo el Real was founded, Spain was in the midst of a literary renaissance known as the *siglo de oro,* or Golden Age. Philip intended that a copy of every book ever published in Spain should be on hand there, as well as editions of every other book that could be obtained. Libraries had always been an important part of monasteries, and this library was to be the most important of all. By 1568, there were already over a thousand books stockpiled at the Escorial, waiting for the library— which occupies the entire second story above the entrance gate and between the monastery and the college — to be completed. Whenever a prominent scholar died, His Majesty sent an agent posthaste to buy the deceased man's best books, and those choice volumes were added to the king's growing collection.

Among other things, Philip was the first Christian king to collect Arabic literature. He took a great interest in Islamic culture, for although he was in many ways a religious bigot he was also a son of the Renais-

To house his superb collection of Greek, Latin, and Arabic manuscripts, Philip added a vast, vaulted library to the monastery. That 175-foot-long chamber is lined with specially designed bookcases of ebony, cedar, orangewood, and walnut — and surmounted by vivid frescoes representing the seven Liberal Arts. The armillary sphere in the foreground is a haunting symbol of Spain's dismantled empire. Behind it stretch dozens of showcases displaying maps, medals, and other mementos of Philip's reign.

sance and educated by humanists. He especially prized Arabic books on medicine and astronomy, and most of the books captured after the battle of Lepanto or confiscated by the Inquisition eventually found their way into the king's collection. From every corner of the known world came books that had been bought by Philip or presented to him. Pending classification, they were retained in a third-story room that later became a dormitory for novices. Librarians and copyists worked continually, and in 1592 when the library itself was finished, the books in Latin, Greek, and Hebrew were installed, under the direction of Fray Sigüenza. Before Philip died, many thousands of books had been catalogued and arranged. They were — and still are — placed in the cases with their spines facing inward and their edges, many of them gilded, exposed to view in the accepted medieval manner.

Herrera designed the library, taking as his model the Laurentian Library in Florence. The bookcases and woodwork are of fine inlaid wood, and the frescoes by Tibaldi are interspersed with grotesques by another Italian artist, Nicolas Granelo. Tibaldi was easily the most prolific of Philip's stable of Italian painters: besides the numerous frescoes in the library, he painted most of those in the Upper Cloister, as well as the lower and upper tiers of the retable behind the high altar. He also repainted or touched up the commissioned works by Federigo Zuccaro and Luca Cambiaso that had failed to please the king.

According to Sigüenza, who knew him well, Tibaldi sometimes used Dürer's works as models, showed the influence of Raphael and Michelangelo, and blamed the fact that his colors were often harsh and monotonous on the inexperienced assistants he was forced to use because of the king's desire to have the work finished as rapidly as possible. Tibaldi worked at the Escorial from 1588 to 1596 and returned to Italy richer by 100,000 escudos and the title of marquis. Unhappily, he did not live to enjoy these rewards but died two months later.

A portrait of Fray Sigüenza hangs in the library. It is the work of the Spanish artist Alonso Sánchez Coello, and it has been called one of the finest Spanish portraits of the age, especially in its composition and color. Another contemporary portraitist of note was Juan Pantoja de la Cruz, a student of Coello who had painted three Spanish monarchs: Charles V, Philip II, and Philip III — the latter two from life. All three paintings are at the Escorial.

On the whole, Philip was more fortunate in the paintings he collected than in those he commissioned. He had his father's collection to build on — including splendid examples of the work of van der Weyden, Dürer, Bosch, and the brothers van Eyck — and he added canvases of the first quality by Titian, Veronese, and Tintoretto. If for nothing else, the Escorial would have been famous for its art collection, and even today — after fires, sackings, and the removal of a number of works to the Prado — it still merits a visit for its paintings alone, many of which have recently been assembled in a suite of small rooms in the section of the Escorial known as the summer palace.

Philip was clearly more interested in embellishing the church and monastery than the palace. However, he did set aside one sixty-yard-long hall adjoining the royal apartments to be decorated with frescoes showing

famous Spanish battles. One entire wall depicts the battle of Higueruela, a Castilian victory over the Moors in 1431. The artists, Granelo, Tavarone, and Castello, worked from a tapestry found packed away in a lumber room in the Alcazar in Segovia. The fresco is said to give a very accurate representation of medieval arms, costumes, and battle formations. The remaining frescoes, executed on separate panels, show the battles of Saint-Quentin and Lepanto, and other military and naval successes of Philip's reign.

The throne room of Europe's most powerful king was remarkably unpretentious. The grandest aspect of the room today is its doors, magnificent examples of German Renaissance marquetry, which were presented to Philip by his father-in-law Emperor Maximilian II. One of these doors leads into the salon where visiting diplomats and ambassadors awaited audience with the king. Another connects with the king's study. From that simple room, seated at a plain wooden desk, Philip commanded half the world. Some of his favorite paintings and art objects surrounded him, among them Hieronymus Bosch's *The Garden of Earthly Delights*, which Philip acquired at auction and which now hangs in the Prado.

This strange painting, which many viewers find disturbing, obscene, and incomprehensible, clearly meant much to Philip and pleased him greatly. It seems a surprising favorite for a prudent and conservative king. In an analysis of the painting, Gilbert Highet has pointed out that for Bosch, hell was the absence of reason. Was this the message in *The Garden of Earthly Delights* that appealed to Philip? No one can be sure what Bosch meant by it, but in Highet's opinion the

artist was trying to show not only that humanity is doomed and damned, but that "the mission of Jesus Christ was perfectly useless. At the very moment when the human and animal world was created, cruelty and sin were part of Paradise. . . . [Mankind] will in the end hand itself over to the powers of darkness and madness. Eternity will be a lunatic asylum." If such had been Philip's view, he would have been obliged to order himself arrested by the Inquisition. Perhaps what the pious king saw in the painting was nothing more than a reminder of the wages of sin and of the absence of reason.

Among the king's favorite possessions was a small bas-relief of Calvary, done in chased silver and set in an ebony frame. An exquisite piece of work — and quite possibly executed by a follower of Benvenuto Cellini — it stands today on the desk in Philip's study. An inscription indicates that it was originally a gift of Pope Gregory XIII to Bianca Capello, Grand Duchess of Tuscany. Like modern rulers and leaders, King Philip was constantly receiving presents from lesser lights who were anxious to ingratiate themselves with him. The things he liked best he added to the Escorial collection; a document is still in existence that enumerates them, and the Calvary is on the list. Bianca Capello, the noblewoman who presented the bas-relief to Philip, was a Venetian beauty whom the Grand Duke of Tuscany, Francesco de' Medici, had married for love rather than because she was a suitable match for him. She undoubtedly thought it prudent to curry favor with the great Spanish sovereign, whose vassal her husband was. Philip plainly liked the present, but whether it warmed his heart toward the donor is not recorded.

Since Bianca Capello's ornate Calvary was a religious object, it merited a place in Philip's apartments. The furnishings themselves were plain, however, and as Fray Sigüenza has written, "not of the best make or wood." The king's bedroom was little more than an alcove between the study and the private aperture that looked into the church. Sigüenza reports:

> The adornment of these rooms or of this honored cell is exceedingly simple and plain. . . . It can be seen that he did not come here to be King but to be one of the most pious of religious persons. The vaulted ceiling is unadorned; the walls, white; the floor, brick; and there is little to see; so great was his modesty as to his personal things. The alcove where he slept was filled on both sides with small images of saints so that no matter which way he turned in bed he received consolation in beholding such excellent company.

Here, at the heart of the most elaborate and costly building erected since ancient times, Philip chose to live and die. And here, if anywhere, we get a sense of him as he really was.

192.

himself splendid: when he went to Guadalajara to meet his French bride in January 1560, he wore a white doublet that was thickly encrusted with pieces of hammered gold; a short, hoodless cape in the French style, embroidered with gold and precious stones; and a black cap festooned with white plumes. His bride, magnificent in cloth of silver and wearing a cross of large diamonds upon her childish bosom, stared at him so long and thoughtfully that Philip finally asked, "What are you looking at? To see if I have any gray hairs?"

Despite the difference in their ages, the thirty-three-year-old bridegroom and the fourteen-year-old bride appear to have fallen in love. When, two years later, Isabella contracted smallpox, Philip threw his characteristic prudence to the winds and hung anxiously about her bedside until she was better. Like her brothers, the short-lived Francis II and Charles IX of France, Isabella had a delicate constitution. The young queen was often ill, and rather than entrust her care to Spanish doctors, Isabella's mother, the formidable Catherine de Médicis, had sent her own personal physician, a clever Italian, along in the bride's entourage. The births of Isabella's two daughters were attended by grave complications. When well, she was gay and fond of games and entertainments — perhaps too much so, wrote a solemn Spanish observer, who added that she was virtuous, kind, honest, and had "an excellent moral character." For Philip, the years between 1560 and 1568, when the Escorial was taking shape and Isabella was his queen, may well have been his happiest.

Philip's son, Don Carlos, was the same age as his stepmother, and a match between them had once been planned. Schiller's famous play, *Don Carlos,* which

Philip's first son, Don Carlos (left), and Isabella of Valois (above) were both fourteen years old when she became the king's third wife, and as a result latter-day gossips frequently linked their names in a supposedly thwarted — and utterly spurious — love affair. In truth, the queen was devoted to Philip, whose miniature she holds in her right hand.

Verdi used as the basis for his opera of the same name, imagines a love affair between the prince and the queen; when wicked Philip discovers it, he causes Don Carlos to be put to death and then hounds his wife into an early grave. Schiller got his idea from sixteenth-century gossip, spread over Europe by Philip's enemies; yet there is no shred of evidence that Isabella felt anything but a pitying kindness for the young man, who was spoiled, frail, and given to temper tantrums. When Don Carlos was seventeen, he fell down a flight of stone steps (on his way, so it was said, to a rendezvous with the porter's daughter), and fractured his skull. When the royal physicians had exhausted their remedies, the body of a revered monk, Fray Diego, dead more than a hundred years, was brought from its resting place in a Madrid church and put into bed beside the prince.

Fray Diego had a reputation for miracles, and many of the faithful thought that his spirit had worked another, for Don Carlos began to recover immediately and was soon up and about again. There was a distressing change in the adolescent prince's personality, however; his temper, never even, became savage. Bizarre stories of his behavior began to circulate: that he had flown into a rage at his bootmaker and forced the unfortunate man to eat a pair of boots, boiled; that he wandered the streets of Madrid with dissolute young men, shouting obscenities at respectable women and even spitting in their faces. Even worse, he appeared to be harboring political ambitions that were dangerous and even treasonable.

The king was spending Epiphany at the Escorial in the winter of 1568 when his half brother, Don Juan of Austria, rode out unannounced from Madrid. In con-fidence he told Philip that Don Carlos was in correspondence with the Dutch rebels and might take it into his muddled head to go to the Netherlands and become their leader. Philip, who loathed decisions, was now called upon to make one as painful as a father or king ever had to make. After days of vacillation, he learned that Don Carlos was on the verge of leaving Spain. Philip roused himself to action. He took a strong guard to the young man's apartments at the Alcazar in Madrid and turned the bedroom into a prison.

From that day, the prince was never seen abroad again. Seven months later he died, apparently from natural causes brought about by alternately starving and gorging himself. Europe buzzed with the rumor that the King of Spain had ordered his son poisoned, but it seems probable that nature mercifully made this decision for him. Don Carlos's instability may have come from his great-grandmother Juana la Loca, from whom he was descended through both parents. Or perhaps it was due to a birth injury — his birth, which killed his mother, had been long and difficult, and from the beginning he had been a difficult child, crying continually and biting his wet-nurses.

In September 1568, a few weeks after the death of Don Carlos, Philip's twenty-two-year-old queen died of the effects of a miscarriage. Although she had failed to accomplish the duty of queens — to provide princes — Isabella had left Philip his two favorite children, Isabella Clara Eugenia, who was the only person in the world he trusted, and the intelligent and lively Catalina Micaela, who was to marry the Duke of Savoy and become an ancestress of the kings of Italy. But these were daughters and Philip was convinced that women should

Death struck the royal household twice in the fall of 1568, leaving Spain without a queen and the king without an heir. Philip's chief consolation during the ensuing months of mourning were the daughters his frail third wife had borne him, Isabella Clara Eugenia (below left) and Catalina Micaela. The tiny infantas, whose classic Spanish beauty is revealed in this study by court painter Sánchez Coello, were to prove a source of joy and comfort to their increasingly burdened father.

63.

not reign. He had vividly before him two examples of incompetent queens — his second wife, Mary Tudor, and another unlucky Mary, the Queen of Scotland. Elizabeth of England could not in justice be called incompetent even by Philip — for she had outmaneuvered him in the cold war between Spain and England — but she was certainly not his idea of a proper queen.

Philip felt obliged to beget a male heir. "Duty flowed in his veins instead of blood," someone has said. In 1570 he took a fourth bride — this time his niece, Anna of Austria, the daughter of his sister and the Emperor Maximilian. Anna was also his cousin once-removed, her imperial grandfather having been the brother of Charles V. She was thus doubly descended from Juana la Loca — but the royal houses of Spain and Austria seem to have had no interest in genetics. A pious, amenable, dull girl half the king's age, Anna fulfilled her purpose by producing four sons in rapid succession. Three died in childhood but one lived to succeed his father on the throne of Spain as Philip III.

Anna of Austria was the only one of Philip's four consorts to spend any length of time at the Escorial. According to Sigüenza, the royal family liked to come there for the summer months and also for religious holidays, at which times their chief delight was in the performance of holy works and visits to the relics. In June 1576, he tells us, the king and queen arrived for the summer, bringing with them their firstborn, Prince Ferdinand. It was the first time the child had left Madrid, and it was not surprising that "the eagle," as Sigüenza calls Philip, should have brought his "fledgling" to the Escorial on his first flight. In summer, "when the sun went down — and it went quickly be-

hind the western mountains — one breathed a cool air that refreshed all that the heat of the day might have put out of tune. The queen and the princes and princesses would come out into the gardens that are all around the royal apartments — so that, as one might say, they could get much fresh air without having to seek for it." Sometimes they made excursions into the surrounding forests and meadows. The king liked to hunt from a carriage, using a crossbow and arrow. In short, ". . . both inside and outside there was for the royal persons a place filled with sweet entertainment."

One of the four little princes, Carlos Lorenzo, was born unexpectedly at a town on the road between Madrid and the Escorial. Not quite two years later, in 1575, he died, and his small body was brought to the Escorial to repose in the royal crypt. From heaven, Sigüenza says, the child "could see, laughing, how little earthly kingdoms are worth." The day after the funeral Prince Diego was born, and he lived to run about the corridors and gardens of the Escorial with his brother, Ferdinand, and a baby sister, Maria. At Easter 1578, the queen observed Maundy Thursday in the great church, "which was a lot for the queen to do, because she was very pregnant with Prince Don Felipe III . . . so that before he was born and from the womb of his mother he began to perform acts of religion and piety in this house."

Alonso Sánchez Coello painted the princes' portraits in the 1570's, and their pinched and large-eyed little faces look out touchingly from the age-dark canvases. The wan complexions and frail physiques of Sánchez Coello's royal subjects are graphic evidence of a tragic fact: Philip's sons were all sickly. Once when Ferdi-

nand seemed to be at death's door in Madrid, the king
sent word to his monks at the Escorial, asking for their
prayers. And when the child began to recover, the
thoughtful king sent a messenger to the Escorial, who
arrived at midnight while the monks were at matins.
He beat loudly upon the door, ". . . and when it was
known who he was, and what happy news he had
brought," writes Sigüenza, "we made a procession
round the cloister, singing a Te Deum Laudamus that
would have put devotion and spirit into the most luke-
warm believer." Prince Ferdinand lived nearly three
years longer and died of a fever at the age of seven.

Although Philip's years with this wife and family
were few, it is pleasing to imagine them all together
at the Escorial in the summer, the children at play
among the bright flowerbeds and Anna and her twenty-
six ladies engaged in needlework before the open windows. According to a Venetian ambassador, Philip was
"very tender toward the queen" during these idyllic
interludes at the Escorial. No matter how busy he was
he visited her apartments every afternoon, and at night
they slept in two low beds, slightly separated but surrounded by a curtain that made them seem to be one.
Sometimes when the king was working at his desk
Anna would sit beside him, and when a letter was finished she would sprinkle it with sand before handing
it to one of the two little infantas, who would carefully
carry it across the room to be sealed by one of her
father's secretaries.

Prince Ferdinand was Philip's most promising son,
and his death in 1578 was one of Philip's most bitter
sorrows. In a letter written to inform his viceroy in
Sicily about the death, the grieving monarch spoke of
the child's "good and gentle nature and great promise
of virtue." But, he added, there must be no period of
mourning, but instead devotional processions, giving
thanks to God and begging him to abate his wrath and
disregard the sins that had been committed against him
by the king and his subjects.

Through these decades, the affairs of state were becoming more and more burdensome, and Philip insisted on carrying the entire weight himself. He had
no favorites, friends, or cronies, and though he sometimes asked for advice he made his own decisions. During the 1560's and early 1570's his advisors were the
Duke of Alba and the Prince of Eboli, two brilliant
men who seldom held the same opinion. Their differ-
ences gave Philip an admirable opportunity to hear an
intelligent view of both sides of a question before
making his own decision.

As has been noted, Philip was no soldier, so that
when it came to actual fighting he had to put someone
else in charge — although, typically, he always managed
to hamper his generals with reams of written instructions. During the early years of Philip's reign the
threatening eastward advance of the Ottoman Turks
was his most worrisome problem. In view of it, the
presence in Spain of thousands of Moriscos, persons of
Arab descent who had nominally accepted Christianity and Spanish rule but whose loyalty was dubious,
seemed a risk to Spain. Philip saw it as his duty to suppress, disperse, or exterminate them. To carry out this
unpleasant operation, Philip chose his twenty-four-
year-old half brother, Don Juan of Austria.

Philip had always hoped that Don Juan would become a monk, but since the young man's inclinations

were neither pacific nor celibate, Philip kindly allowed him to take the field instead — and there Charles V's illegitimate son soon showed the qualities of a great commander: bravery, cunning ruthlessness, and charisma. That Don Juan was also reckless and overly ambitious was not then apparent, and when Spain formed a Holy League with Venice and the pope against the Turks in 1571, Philip put Don Juan in command of the Christian forces: 80,000 men, mostly Spaniards, in more than 200 ships. It was a formidable array, but the sultan had an even larger one — plus the profound psychological advantage of never having been defeated in battle.

For most of the preceding decade the Turks had been harassing the once-powerful Venetian Republic, and only that summer they had taken from her the island of Cyprus. Philip had no particular regard for the Venetians, who were known for lying and double-dealing, but they were a valuable buffer in the eastern Mediterranean and for that reason alone Philip felt compelled to support them.

Under wind-tossed banners of cross and crescent, the two juggernauts faced each other at the mouth of the Greek gulf of Lepanto on October 7, 1571. As history records, the battle fought there resulted in an overwhelming victory for the Christians. After fighting that lasted five hours, all but fifty of the three hundred Ottoman ships had been lost. The galley that carried the treasure of the Ottoman fleet was in Christian hands, and Ali Pasha, the sultan's commander, had been killed and his head stuck on a pike to encourage the Christians and to drive the infidel to despair.

The Christian casualties were great — 7,650 killed

and about the same number wounded, but the Turkish losses were in excess of 30,000. Don Juan wanted to follow the fleeing ships all the way to Constantinople, overthrow the sultan, and reestablish the Byzantine Empire with himself as emperor. The ever-wary Philip refused to permit this or any other advantage to be taken of the victory, however, for he knew that the Turks were still formidable in spite of their defeat, and by now he was also aware of his half brother's reckless lust for power. Thus the greatest gain at Lepanto was psychological: it proved that the formidable Turks could be defeated and it freed Europe from a dread that had lasted since the fall of Constantinople more than a century earlier.

Three weeks after the battle, on All Hallows' Eve, Philip was attending vespers at the Escorial when a courtier burst in and blurted out the news of the victory. Philip's reaction was typical: his face betrayed no emotion, and after listening to the barest details, he turned back to the vesper service. When it was over, he requested that a Te Deum be sung. He then left the church and returned to his study, where he at last allowed himself to hear the whole glorious story.

When Spain learned of the triumph at Lepanto, Don Juan of Austria became the nation's hero. Spanish soldiers would have followed the young commander anywhere, and his ambitions became grandiose and consequently dangerous. Thwarted in his plan to take Constantinople, Don Juan next conceived the idea of carving out a great empire in North Africa, one that would be nominally ruled by Philip but actually governed by himself. Philip again refused to cooperate, this time pleading low funds. The truth was that the king wanted to spike his half brother's grand design, for Philip could see that Don Juan was a great asset to the nation, but one that the king must not allow to get out of hand. After keeping the hero of Lepanto idle and powerless for nearly five years, Philip finally appointed him governor-general of the Spanish Netherlands, where the political situation had been going from bad to worse.

From 1566 to 1573, Philip had allowed the Duke of Alba to govern the Netherlands with an iron hand, executing thousands of rebels and heretics. Convinced by 1573 that Alba's policy was intensifying rather than ending rebellion, Philip turned to the milder, more tolerant policy that the Prince of Eboli had been urging for years. Eboli died soon thereafter, and Philip replaced Alba as governor-general with Luis de Zúñiga y Requeséns, an experienced diplomat. Requeséns sought to make a dramatic beginning by announcing a general pardon, but its effect was negated by a mutiny and riot among Spanish troops, who had been unpaid for months.

A much worse riot, known to history as "The Spanish Fury," occurred in Antwerp in 1577. More than eight thousand innocent citizens were murdered — men, women, and children, Protestants and Catholics alike. The immediate result was the unification of all seventeen provinces of the Low Countries in an intense determination to drive the Spaniards out. Thus it was into an increasingly hectic atmosphere that Philip sent the warrior-hero Don Juan with instructions to bring about peace and harmony.

Don Juan had a secretary named Juan de Escobedo, who had been hand-picked by Philip as a person likely to influence the young man in ways of prudence and wisdom. Escobedo had been brought up in the household of the Prince of Eboli, as Philip's own secretary, Antonio Pérez, had been. In the sixteenth century, a ruler's secretary was not only a scribe but a person of considerable political knowledge and sagacity; always at his master's elbow, he was privy to virtually every state secret. (The modern title of secretary for persons of high government rank originated in the days when a man who performed secretarial duties for a king also had a hand on the reins of government.) Antonio Pérez, shrewd and hardworking, was eminently qualified for his job in all ways except one: he was corruptible. And he was to involve the king in a most unsavory scandal.

It began in the year of the seven sevens, 1577, the year against which the astrologers had warned Philip. Don Juan, restless and disillusioned in Flanders, launched an expensive and unauthorized military thrust against the rebel forces, and then sent his secretary, Escobedo, to the Escorial with an appeal for money. Escobedo, it appears, had by this time forgotten his role as watchdog over Don Juan. He was thoroughly in the thrall of the fascinating prince and eager to forward Don Juan's latest visionary scheme — which was to conquer England, depose Elizabeth, and set Mary Queen of Scots upon the throne with himself beside her as king-consort. Together they would rule over England, Scotland, and the Netherlands.

The two secretaries — Pérez and Escobedo — were an unattractive pair and knew too much about each other. Pérez was a purveyor of state secrets who had regularly sold Don Juan top-secret information from Philip's desk. Escobedo, who was aware of Pérez's corruptibility, also knew that Philip's secretary and the widow of the Prince of Eboli were engaged in political intrigue and were even in communication with certain Dutch rebels. Pérez realized that he must silence Escobedo, and he may have persuaded the king that the man was a kind of evil genius, capable of goading Don Juan to foolish and traitorous actions, and that in the national interest he should be eliminated. At any rate, in March 1578, after three unsuccessful attempts to poison Escobedo, Pérez at last succeeded in having him assassinated on the dark streets of Madrid.

Whether Philip ordered or tacitly allowed the assassination — or even knew anything about it — will never be known. But his subsequent kid-glove handling of Pérez arouses the suspicion that the secretary had documentary evidence hidden away that would have inculpated the king.

If Philip did order the assassination, he soon regretted it. In the months following Escobedo's death he became convinced that both Pérez and the Princess of Eboli were traitors — and after sending for one of his father's former right-hand counselors, Cardinal de Granvelle, Philip had Pérez arrested and the Princess of Eboli confined to one room of her provincial palace, where she remained until she died many years later. Pérez languished in jail for several years and then was tried for misconduct in office and sentenced to ten years. He escaped, was recaptured, and eventually stood trial for the murder of Escobedo. This time he managed to escape by changing clothes with his wife when she visited him in his cell. He made his way to Aragon and eventually to France, where he lived until 1611,

selling every secret he knew — and perhaps some he fabricated — to the French or English, whichever bid higher. In the end, all his secrets were hopelessly outdated, and he died in poverty and obscurity.

The Pérez affair made Philip loath to trust those around him. As one of the perspicacious Venetians wrote some years later, "He never says anything without having thought profoundly about it first. He moderates his passions, and answers pleasantly; hides his thoughts, and one never knows if he is influenced or annoyed by anyone until that person is given a reward or punishment. . . . He guards his actions with marvelous gravity and they say he never gives an opinion in public." Someone else, less sympathetic, observed, "The king's dagger follows close upon his smile."

In the late summer of 1578, the thirty-two-year-old Don Juan fell ill with a fever and died in a Flemish barracks. Philip had his body brought to the Escorial and buried with all royal honors by the side of their father. The prince's remains, now in the Pantheon of the Infantes, lie beneath a lifelike marble effigy made during the nineteenth century. It has been known to move lady tourists to tears and some have even kissed the marble lips. Although Don Juan's father was an emperor, his mother was a simple German burgher girl — and Philip never quite let him forget it. But here, among the dust of his haughty, highborn relatives, he is at last their equal, and still seems to weave the spell that enchanted women, bound his soldiers to him, and caused Fray Sigüenza to call him "a new Scipio, in whom were joined virtues seldom found in captains."

Two months before Don Juan's death, another family catastrophe caused far-reaching changes for Philip

The two great armadas that met in the Greek gulf of Lepanto on October 7, 1571, were mismatched in both size and experience. The Ottoman navy, flying the white crescent of the Sublime Porte, was superior in both respects to the seaborne army of the Holy League, led by Don Juan. Thus, when the two fleets met in hand-to-hand combat (above), few could have predicted the result:

25,000 Turks dead, 5,000 more taken prisoner, and 250 Ottoman warships captured or sunk. Turkish officials disdainfully suggested that Don Juan had merely "cut off the beard of the Sultan," but the battle of Lepanto was more than a trimming: the Ottoman threat to Europe had been curtailed for decades, and the myth of Turkish invincibility on the high seas had been destroyed forever.

and for Spain. Earlier that summer, Philip's nephew Sebastian, King of Portugal, had led the flower of Portuguese manhood into Morocco on a sort of latter-day crusade. Philip had warned Sebastian against the enterprise, for he was certain that the Moors could outfight the Portuguese, and the unlikely event of a Portuguese victory would only attract the Turks to the western Mediterranean in aid of their coreligionists. But Sebastian, who was young, arrogant, and a religious fanatic, would listen to no one. Filled with anachronistic crusading zeal, he led his troops into the Moroccan hinterland, where they were virtually annihilated on August 4 at the grim battle of Alcazarquivir. Sebastian himself died, along with thousands of hapless soldiers under his ill-fated command.

Philip was celebrating the feast of Saint Lawrence at the Escorial when he learned of the disastrous battle. "He could not disguise his grief," writes Sigüenza, "even though he had been prepared for the blow, believing that such an ill-considered venture could have no good end." The king retired to his oratory after receiving the news and sent word to the prior to order special disciplines and prayers. A short time later he left for Madrid.

> Going out through a secret door in the garden, almost alone, and obviously deeply saddened; undoubtedly this was . . . one of the harshest blows that he and even the whole of Spain had received in many years and from which such great damage resulted that it can never be mended. . . . From that day to this the king has never been without an inventory of miserable tragedies that follow one upon another.

An aged uncle of Sebastian's, a cardinal, took the Portuguese throne, but he died a little more than a year later, naming Philip as his heir. There was another claimant, an illegitimate cousin with a considerable following, and his existence prompted Philip to act with uncharacteristic decisiveness: before the rival could assert himself, Philip journeyed to Portugal and had himself crowned. He took the queen with him, and shortly after their arrival they both caught influenza, which was rampant that year all over Europe. Philip recovered, but Anna died.

In order to ensure the annexation of Portugal, Philip tarried in that country for two years. His children remained in Spain, sometimes at the Escorial. He wrote to them often, showing a side of himself that those who hated him would have found unbelievable:

(Lisbon, 10 July, 1581): You do well to keep me informed about the health of your brothers. I devoutly hope that the elder is already perfectly recovered, and the younger as well. I think the fevers must have been caused by the heat, which must have ceased by now, for here we hardly feel it and today has been rather cool. . . . The peaches arrived in such a state that one would not have known what they were if you had not written me; so I could not enjoy them; which I regret very much, because coming from the little garden beneath your window they would have given me great pleasure. Here in some places they have little gardens that they call *alegretes,* which are not bad. We will bring home the plans, although I don't know where we could create one.

Here there is not much to tell you about, except that yesterday my nephew and I went to mass at the Dominican convent. . . . In the afternoon came two

Moorish princes who are staying here, an uncle and his nephew, the latter still a child, with many Moors on foot and on horseback. This morning a fleet left here of fourteen or fifteen galleons and *navires* and caravelles with a thousand Spaniards and a thousand Germans. . . . This fleet is now before Belem, waiting for a favorable wind. This afternoon we went to see the flagship; there was a bit of wind; and seasickness. . . . After we had reviewed the ships, as well as the troops on board them, we came home under sail, in order to profit by the wind which was blowing in that direction; until today we have always gone by oar. It was almost nightfall when we arrived. Before leaving the galleon, we were present at the salute that they are accustomed to have on Saturdays, so that my nephew could see how they do it; most of it was performed by a group of minstrels, slaves from the galleon, who played various instruments and acquitted themselves very well. I don't know whether you are aware that, having no one here who knows how to play the organ, I sent for Cabezón [the king's official musician]. Magdalena came aboard the galleon where I was today; I think she was a little seasick.

Philip's serving-woman, Magdalena, who was a dwarf and perhaps a little simple, figures in many of the king's letters. He seems to have been especially fond of her, for he later made her a serving-woman to the infantas and he refers to her with special tenderness.

Magdalena has a great liking for strawberries and I for nightingales, although I hear only a few now, and them from one of my windows. . . . They write to me that your little brother has cut a tooth; it seems to me that he is very slow about it, since he is already three years old, for it is the anniversary of his baptism, as you will remember; and I am in doubt whether it is two or three years — I believe three — but I believe he must be as handsome as you say.

Magdalena has been very displeased with me since I wrote to you because I did not scold Luis Tristan for a dispute they had in the presence of my nephew, which I did not hear, but I believe she started it, and treated him very badly. She goes about very angry with me, saying that she wants to go away and that she is going to kill him, but I believe that by tomorrow she will have forgotten it.

In 1583 Philip returned to the Escorial, and he never left Spain again. His faithful monks must have been shocked at his appearance. Since his illness, his beard had turned white and he had aged significantly. Lonely and full of sorrows, he at once plunged into the one pleasure that had never failed him: building, improving, embellishing, and elaborating the Escorial.

V

Dissent at Home, Defeat at Sea

"Men and events are made what they are by the character of the age to which they belong," the English historian G. N. Clark once observed. If all of the sixteenth-century world had been Christian and Roman Catholic — or if religion had not been the supreme preoccupation of the age — Philip II of Spain might not have been a religious fanatic and bigot. There would have been no need for a Spanish Inquisition, nor for a Council of Trent. And there might well have been no Escorial, which has been called the monument of the Counter-Reformation, "an expression in stone of Catholicism in Spain; an answer, solid and unified, to the disintegration of the Christian universe."

For Philip, the vast monastery-palace was the home of God on earth. In his view, which was the view of all who followed Rome, the Protestant threat called for standing firm within a spiritual Escorial and destroying those who sought to breach its walls. It comes as no surprise therefore that one of Philip's first acts when he returned to Spain in 1559 was to attend an auto-da-fé, a public trial and condemnation of masses of heretics that was held in the plaza in Valladolid. Whether the king stayed on into the night to see the condemned burned at the stake is not recorded.

An English account of Philip's last days, published in 1599, notes: "It is remarkable that he was arrived to that state of hypocritical insensibility and delusion that he thought all his barbarities, treachery and treasons were doing God service and that himself was ready to depart this life in the favour of God." The Protestant Englishman who wrote those lines had conveniently overlooked the fact that "barbarities" were also committed in God's name in England and everywhere else. Queen Elizabeth

had burned English Catholics, beheaded her cousin the Queen of Scotland, and allowed savage persecutions of Irish Catholics as well. The times were grim and Philip belonged to his times.

One of the grimmest aspects of life in sixteenth-century Spain was the all-powerful Inquisition. Its importance in the history of Spain at this time cannot be exaggerated, particularly as it was one of the two institutions that affected the lives of all Spaniards (the other was the monarchy). So powerful was this religious tribunal that in 1559 it even dared attempt to imprison the Archbishop of Toledo, the head of the Spanish church. Philip favored and abetted the Inquisition, which he believed was necessary for the welfare of the country; however, he did not invent it. The idea of forming a religious court to root out heresy had been conceived in the Middle Ages, and over the centuries there had been inquisitions in most European countries.

Spain's court was first convened by Ferdinand and Isabella as a purely Spanish body, not subject to the pope. It had its own Index of Forbidden Books and, until Rome strenuously objected, it sold its own indulgences. On the whole it was more zealous in its pursuit of heresy than was the pope himself. Both Charles V and Philip II gave it full support so that during the sixteenth century the Inquisition was like a giant spider whose web stretched over all of Spain and her colonies. Inquisitorial spies were everywhere; no one led a private life. A man might suddenly be arrested, stripped of his property, and cast into a dungeon from which there was no appeal except to the king — and the king rarely intervened. The accused might languish in prison for years, deprived of the sacraments and subject to harsh treatment. Torture was used, but only as a last resort.

After being tried — not before a tribunal but in a series of interrogations — the prisoner received his sentence: it might be a reprimand, exile, scourging, imprisonment, or a turn in the galleys. In a number of cases the sentence was death by burning at the stake. Serious offenders had to appear at an auto-da-fé, or public ceremony of penance, where those who had received the death sentence were granted the favor of being strangled before their bodies were burned — if they were judged properly penitent.

Not even the most respected Spanish citizens were safe from the vast Inquisitorial intelligence network. As a young man Fray Sigüenza had been tried and sentenced to three months' seclusion. Saint Ignatius of Loyola, founder of the Jesuit order, was twice imprisoned by the Inquisition, as were several of Spain's brilliant scientists and philosophers. Others, like the great Erasmian scholar Juan Luis Vives, prudently chose to live abroad. Even Saint Teresa of Avila was accused of misconduct, and one of her books was placed on the Index. In this particular case Philip intervened, but only because he had corresponded with Teresa and was in sympathy with her goals and opinions. Moreover, he had an almost slavish respect for persons in holy orders, from the greatest cardinal down to the humble brothers who prayed for him at the Escorial.

Saint Teresa, born at Avila in 1515, was a Carmelite nun. When she was nearly forty years old she suddenly began to have visions, and partly as a result of them she determined to found a house of descalzas, or barefoot, Carmelite sisters who would adhere to the original, strict rules of the order. The pope gave his permission, but the parent order objected strenuously, as did the townspeople of Avila. The situation turned into a cause célèbre and came to the attention of the king. With his protection, Teresa was allowed to establish a small convent at Avila. She spent the rest of her life journeying about Spain, founding more houses in spite of continued bitter opposition from the Carmelites who preferred more relaxed rules.

The king and the nun had much in common. Both were champions of the Counter-Reformation, and both were anxious to suppress all the excesses and worldliness that had crept into the church, in order to make it strong, austere, and unbending. Both wanted to destroy its enemies, build more churches and monasteries, and restore those sacked by Protestants in northern Europe — and both were indefatigable wielders of the pen.

The same instincts prompted Teresa to found her sisterhood and Philip to build his "dwelling for God on earth," and coincidentally, Teresa began her convent in the same year — 1562 — in which Philip cleared the site of the Escorial. A modern hagiographer has warned against extending the parallel indefinitely:

The work of Saint Teresa [is] not a rigid monument [like the king's] . . . but a living one that grows through the centuries and after four hundred years covers all the earth. . . . Saint Teresa and Philip II [were] renowned defenders of the Catholic Church. . . . If in this building he recorded his catholicism in stone, in the protection he gave to Saint Teresa he showed a charity that endures inseparable from her glory.

Saint Teresa died in 1582 while the king was in Portugal. According to tradition, her grave exuded an odor of violets — and when her body was exhumed

nine months later, it had not begun to decompose. A
monk severed one hand from the nun's corpse, and it
was soon said to perform miracles. Teresa's fame as a
saint spread rapidly after 1583, and she was canonized
in 1622. Philip obviously believed that Teresa was no
ordinary woman, and after her death he collected as
many of her manuscripts as his agents could find. One
of these was her autobiography, which she called "my
soul" and which had been under examination by the
Inquisition at Toledo for ten years. These documents
were kept under lock and key in the library at the Escorial, and Philip carried the key as long as he lived.
About the middle of the eighteenth century the monks
moved Teresa's papers to the chamber of relics, but
today they are back in the library, where a few pages
are exhibited in a glass case.

Philip delighted in saintly lore and legend, and one
of his greatest pleasures at the Escorial was in forming
an enormous collection of holy relics. The first ship-
ment — which included relics donated by the king's
sister Maria, Queen of Hungary, and others acquired
by personal representatives of the king — arrived in
1574, before the church of San Lorenzo el Real was
even finished. Sigüenza records that when Philip came
to the monastery in the spring of 1586 to celebrate Holy
Week with the monks, as was his custom, he brought:

> Jewels for the altar and sacristy and very precious
> relics, including an ankle bone of the glorious martyr
> Lawrence . . . and the head of the very glorious
> martyr-prince Hermenegildo of Spain. . . . These
> things the king wanted to place here so that he could
> enjoy his church, the work of his hands (those who
> have never built anything cannot understand what a

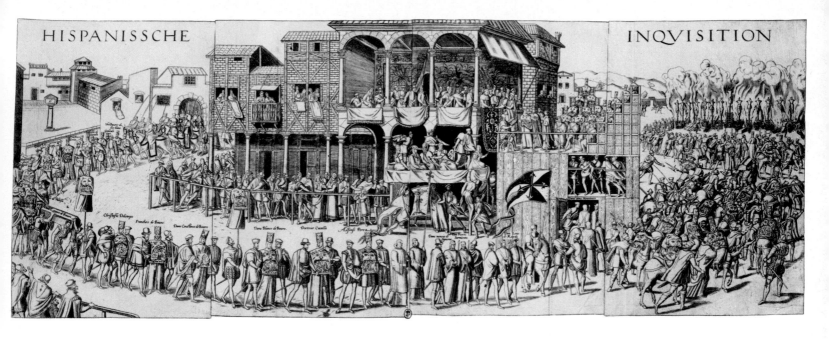

great desire this is, especially when the work is so illustrious and so beautiful).

During important ceremonies at the Escorial, certain relics were shown to the people from the windows of the choir. Indeed, the only respite the brothers had from their strictly ordered rounds of prayer and work were these long, complicated ceremonies involving masses, Te Deums, Misereres, processions, and relic-viewing. The monks apparently never tired of such rites, and neither did the king. He would sit for hours in his corner of the choir, in a stall that he often shared with his little son, Philip.

Certain of these ceremonies, such as the dedication of the church and the reinterment of the royal corpses, went on for days. When the pope sent Queen Anna the special honor of the Golden Rose, the rites were long and intricate; and they were all repeated a few years later when the Infanta Isabella Clara Eugenia was also accorded a Golden Rose. Then there were the regular saints' days and feast days of the church calendar, the fasting and contrition of Holy Week, and the endless offering of masses for the royal dead — to say nothing of royal funerals and memorial services held in honor of deceased royal relatives in other countries. Elaborate obsequies were held for Mary Queen of Scots as soon as word reached the Escorial of her execution. From the scaffold, Mary had sent Philip a ring. He entrusted it to Fray Sigüenza (at that time Keeper of the Relics) with instructions that it be placed among the bones of the saints, "for [the king] had great faith that she was a glorious martyr and was with God in Heaven." Philip continued to take part in his beloved ceremonies until he was on his deathbed. When he could no longer

walk in processions or kneel at the altar, he had himself carried to the church in a chair.

The holy relics were kept in locked cupboards in a large room back of the altar, each housed in a reliquary so magnificently jeweled, carved, or enameled as to make this room alone one of the great treasure houses of Europe. During the last decade of his life, Philip often visited the room — sometimes alone, sometimes accompanied by his son and daughter. Sigüenza describes a typical visit:

> There he would ask me . . . to show him such and such a relic. When I took it in my hands, before I could wrap it in silk or linen the very pious king would genuflect, taking off his hat or cap, and kiss it in my very hands. . . . His children would imitate him. . . . This happened to us alone and in secret in that holy room; it should be shouted from the rooftops for the confusion of heretics and other lukewarm Christians.

When the church was consecrated in 1595, certain of the most revered relics were placed in the high altar — among them relics of Saint Lawrence, the twelve Apostles, and Saint Stephen — and indulgences were granted to all those who might thenceforth visit them on the anniversary of the consecration. Two years later the relic collection was greatly augmented by the arrival of four packing cases filled with relics collected in Germany by the king's agents. Because of the danger that they might fall into the hands of heretics, they had been brought to Spain secretly. Leaving Cologne on December 30, 1596, and "passing through a thousand dangers among mountains and valleys, cliffs, boulders, marshes, rivers and snows, a diversity of people and towns, escaping from a thousand dangerous encoun-

A detail (left) from Francisco Ricci's panoramic view of a giant auto-da-fé that overflowed the main plaza in his native Madrid underscores the ecclesiastical pomp and popular fervor that surrounded these essentially repellent spectacles. In time, special tunics were devised to enable onlookers to distinguish penitents (near right) from heretics (far right) bound for the stake.

ters with heretics," they arrived safely in Milan in less than a month — a miraculously short time considering the distance, the era, and the obvious hazards. From Milan they were taken to Genoa and placed on a ship for Spain, "leaving behind them on the sea many ships that had sailed before the one that carried them, to the amazement of the sailors — there was never such a favorable wind. . . ."

When the relics finally reached the Escorial, there was, of course, an extensive ceremony for welcoming and installing them. In honor of the occasion the boys of the school and the monks composed "all manner of verses, sonnets, songs, Castilian couplets, devotional and witty epigrams in Latin, and very loving lyric poetry" and posted them on the pillars and doors outside the church. Philip rewarded the poets by requesting copies of all these works "so that they could be read to him slowly — and this was no small gesture, for he did not care much for poetry."

Sigüenza's chronicle provides a careful catalogue of the relics collected by Philip. Among the particularly valuable items were pieces of the True Cross and one of its nails, a hair of Christ's beard, a thorn from the Crown of Thorns, and a bit of a linen handkerchief used by Mary at the foot of the Cross and bearing traces of her tears. There were also the entire bodies of several early Christian martyrs, including that of Saint Maurice, whose martyrdom El Greco had depicted for Philip. Among the 103 heads was that of Saint Jerome ("a healthy, mature, and solemn head"), acquired from a convent in Cologne at the king's special command in order to preserve it from possible desecration by heretics. Another head was identified as

that of Saint Lawrence, but the king "always understood that this was not certain." He was, however, satisfied as to the authenticity of an arm of Saint Lawrence that was encased in an ancient silver reliquary.

Saint Martin, the apostle Bartholomew, and Mary Magdalene were represented in the arm collection — and as for such relics as fingers, toes, and small joints, this category was so extensive that only three well-known saints were *not* represented: Saint Joseph, Saint John the Baptist, and Saint James (the last being preserved entire at Santiago de Compostela in northwestern Spain). Philip's successors added to the collection and there are now more than 7,000 relics at the Escorial, including 10 bodies, 144 heads, and 306 limbs.

Although Philip was one of the most devout Christian kings who ever lived, he was also a statesman, and when religion and the political benefit of Spain came into conflict he showed himself very much of this world. Largely as a result of having run head-on into the temporal interests of the Vatican, both Philip and his father endured excommunication during most of the papacy of Paul IV, from 1555 to 1559. Despite the awful threat of eternal hellfire, Philip remained steadfast to his political purpose in Italy, which was to prevent France from gaining a foothold and to limit the pope's temporal power. Paul IV, a Neapolitan who was over eighty when he came to the Holy See, had always hated the Spanish for their domination of his native kingdom. But when the Spanish army under the Duke of Alba defeated the French and Vatican forces at Civitella and marched into Rome in September 1557, the pope accepted the inevitable. To quote Sir Charles Petrie in his *Philip II of Spain:*

Elizabeth I's England, long a thorn in Philip's side, became the target of his unbridled wrath when the Protestant queen (left) ordered the execution of her Catholic rival, Mary Queen of Scots. Angered by Elizabeth's sub-rosa assistance to the Dutch rebels, and shocked by her elimination of Mary, Philip gathered the mightiest naval force in history for an all-out attack on the island kingdom. The stunning setback his armada suffered at English hands is celebrated on the satirical playing cards at right, which show Medina-Sidonia, the Spanish admiral, as the knave of clubs.

Alba made a public entrance into Rome, and when he reached the Vatican he fell on his knees before the Pope, asking that he might be pardoned for the offence of bearing arms against the Church. Paul readily granted the required absolution, and asked the Viceroy to lunch with him. . . . Yet nothing could obscure the fact that henceforth Italy, including the States of the Church, was to be a Spanish satellite.

Paul forgave the Duke of Alba, but he was implacable against the duke's master. However, after Paul's death in 1559, Philip engineered the election of his own papal candidate, who as Pius IV immediately rescinded the excommunications of Charles and Philip. Toward the end of his life, Philip was excommunicated again for a short period, this time for undue interference in papal elections.

Like Cardinal Richelieu after him, Philip could accommodate himself to Protestants when he thought it politically expedient. In much the same way that the United States does business with the Soviet Union while remaining unalterably opposed to communism, Philip fought heresy in the Netherlands with terrifying vigor while advising his second wife, the Catholic Mary of England, to rule with tolerance and avoid making Protestant martyrs. Later, when the pope wanted to excommunicate Queen Elizabeth, Philip intervened twice — not because he thought she did not deserve it but to prevent retaliatory persecutions of English Catholics and to avoid stirring up English public opinion against Spain. Philip was highly unpopular in England and was sure to be blamed, along with Spain in general, for the excommunication.

Both Philip and Elizabeth were anxious to avoid war between their two countries and did so for nearly thirty years — but they were on a collision course, for their interests conflicted in both the Old and New worlds. Philip was particularly anxious to end English assistance to the Netherlands. By striking at England, he hoped to isolate the Dutch rebels and bring the uprising to a quick and favorable conclusion.

When, in March 1587, word reached the Escorial that Elizabeth had executed her prisoner the Queen of Scotland, Philip at last began to listen to the advisers who had long been pressing him to proceed against England. In a letter written about this time, he said that he believed Mary to be the most suitable instrument for leading England and Scotland back to the Catholic faith. "But since God in His wisdom has ordained otherwise, He will raise up other instruments for the triumph of His cause." In truth Philip had never wanted Mary to triumph over Elizabeth because her sympathies were entirely French; had she become Queen of England, she would undoubtedly have favored France over Spain and upset the shaky balance of power. But with Mary no longer a factor, Philip could plan to conquer England and even perhaps rule the country himself by placing his daughter on the throne.

In his usual cautious and secretive manner, Philip began in the spring of 1587 to lay plans for a gigantic move against England. The Marquis of Santa Cruz, a veteran of Lepanto and the logical leader for such an enterprise, remarked privately at the time that the king seemed to have *pie de plomo* (lead feet). Some time previously Santa Cruz had sent to the Escorial a detailed plan for an armada of 510 ships and more than 90,000 men. Philip proceeded to cut these numbers in

The 2^d Squadron ruled by Sr Francis Drake

The Army of 20000 Souldiers laid along ŷ Southern Coast of England.

Don Alphonso Duke of Medina, Cheife Comander of ŷ Spanish Fleete & John Martin Recaldẹ a great Seaman.

Severall strange Weapons taken from the Spaniard which were provide to destroy ŷ English

half — and then worked out a strategy whereby the Spanish fleet would sail into the English Channel, effect a meeting with a large army under the command of the Duke of Parma, and ferry those troops from Flanders to the English coast. Both Santa Cruz and Parma advised their monarch that such a plan was unworkable, but Philip was determined to do things his own way; he was convinced that his way was God's way and that he was leading a latter-day crusade.

"Philip chose to regulate everything," J. A. Froude observes in his essay, *The Spanish Story of the Armada.* "The smallest thing and the largest seemed to occupy him equally." From the Escorial to the harbors of Portugal, where the great fleet was slowly being assembled, came instructions on such subjects as the amount of salt fish and bacon to be provided for the men. And because the voyage of the armada against England was a holy expedition, there was to be no swearing or gambling. Whores were ordered out of the ports and extra priests were brought in so that every man could confess and receive absolution before the fleet sailed.

In February 1588, all seemed in readiness. Then, suddenly, Admiral Santa Cruz died — and the entire expedition was delayed while Philip pondered over his successor. The choice was a strange one: the Duke of Medina-Sidonia, who had neither the experience nor the ambition for such a task. "My health is bad," he wrote Philip, "and from my small experience of the water I know that I am always seasick and likely to catch cold. . . . The expedition is on such a scale and the object is of such high importance that the person at the head of it ought to understand navigation and sea-fighting, and I know nothing of either."

But Philip refused to change his mind. He apparently believed that if he sent enough written instructions, any fool could follow them. "If I was less occupied at home," he wrote, "I would accompany the fleet myself and I should be certain that all would go well." He was past sixty then, gouty, and in frail health; in any case, it seems unlikely, given his temperament, that he would ever have chosen to fill the job into which he was thrusting Medina-Sidonia.

At its peak, the armada consisted of 130 ships, 8,066 sailors, and 21,621 soldiers. The number of ships is misleading, for only about half or perhaps two-thirds of them were effective fighters. The rest were either very small and poorly armed or were lumbering troop transports. By the time they finally sailed in May 1588, there had been so many delays that the ships' stores had gone bad and thousands of men became ill. Storms off the Portuguese coast scattered the fleet, and Medina-Sidonia decided to put into port in the north of Spain, take on fresh supplies, and start again. This he was finally able to do in mid-July, and he made his first contact with the English near Plymouth some eight days later.

The English ships were lighter and more easily maneuvered, and they harassed the Spanish cruelly. But Medina-Sidonia was under orders from his king not to give battle until after the rendezvous with Parma, and consequently the armada held to its tight defensive formation and proceeded up the English Channel as far as Calais, where it dropped anchor. There Medina-Sidonia received the disastrous news that Parma, who was blockaded by both Dutch and English ships, would be unable to keep his appointment with the armada.

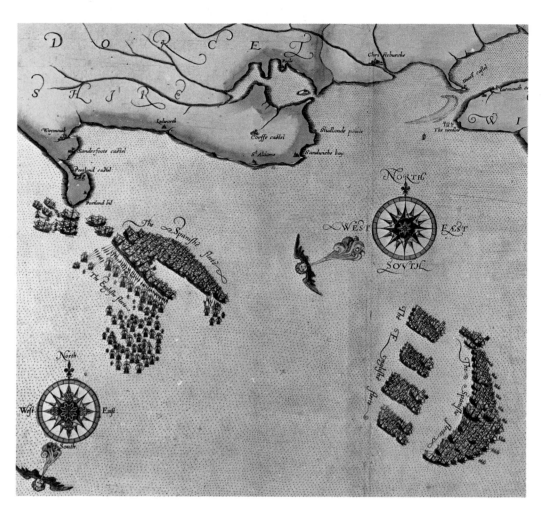

When Philip II's "Enterprise against England" — as he dubbed the 130-ship armada assembled for the express purpose of deposing Elizabeth I and restoring Catholicism to her island kingdom — finally set sail, it did so under the worst of auspices. The normally indecisive king appeared undaunted by the successive disasters that beset his forces as they gathered in the Spanish port of La Coruña, but events themselves seemed to substantiate the darkest forebodings. Santa Cruz, the Lepanto veteran who was chosen to lead the enterprise, died unexpectedly, and his post was reluctantly filled by the Duke of Medina-Sidonia, who had no naval experience, a proclivity for seasickness, and a marked distaste for the whole endeavor. Gale winds, tainted victuals, and a daring foray spearheaded by Sir Francis Drake combined to prevent the fleet from sailing until May 20, 1588. Even then the armada's progress was painfully slow, and Medina-Sidonia's command did not reach the southern coast of England until July 12. As Augustine Ryther's delicately colored contemporary engraving (above) indicates, the Spanish fleet, pursued by an equal number of English vessels under the command of Lord Howard of Effingham, arrived off Portland Bill on July 21 after several days of inconclusive dueling. Re-forming the broad crescent that had rendered them invulnerable, the Spaniards swept across the English Channel to Calais, where they were supposed to rendezvous with the Duke of Parma's seasoned army. Parma's troops had indeed arrived from the Netherlands, but the commander lacked the necessary flat-bottom boats to ferry his waiting troops across to England. While Medina-Sidonia pondered, the English struck: eight ships, including Drake's own vessel, the Thomas, were packed to the gunwales with kindling, set afire, and cut adrift. As they bore down on the armada (left), the Spaniards panicked, slipped anchor, and stood out to sea. The impregnable crescent had been broken. Harried by Howard's ships and scattered by "a Protestant wind," the remains of Philip's once-proud armada drifted north along the Dutch coast. The battle had been brief and the damage relatively minor, but the Glorious Enterprise against Elizabeth's England was finished.

In addition, he was short on troop transports and he lacked a fighting escort.

While Medina-Sidonia was deciding what to do next, the English launched eight fire-ships against the anchored enemy fleet. Caught unaware by this unfamiliar tactic, the Spaniards cut their cables in panic and lost their important defensive formation. A decisive battle followed off the French town of Gravelines, a clash in which several Spanish ships were lost or disabled. In disarray and unable to return to Spain the way they had come, the Spanish fled to the north, heading around Scotland and Ireland in order to reach home. More ships were lost on this voyage, which was fraught with unseasonably violent storms, than had succumbed to the English in the Channel. In the end, fewer than two-thirds of the original fleet and only about 10,000 exhausted men (including Medina-Sidonia) managed to find their way home.

Philip spent a grim summer at the Escorial. All over Spain, the "great enterprise" against England had brought about an upsurge of religious fervor. According to Sigüenza, the churches were crowded and the usually boisterous Festival of Saint John at the end of June was "more like Holy Week." At the monastery of the Escorial, the monks did extraordinary penances. Philip often attended the services they held in the dead of the night, or knelt in his private oratorio where he could hear the chanting. But even with all this, Fray Sigüenza writes, "that thing happened which we all know and bewail." In his judgment the defeat was the worst that had happened to Spain in more than six hundred years, and he added that the "most shameful and painful [aspect] was that our true religion lost much credit with the perfidious enemy, who believed and wrote that God was on their side. . . ."

It is said that when Philip, in his Escorial study, received the news of the defeat and flight of the armada, he displayed the same stoicism with which he had greeted the news of the victory at Lepanto: "I give thanks to God by whose hand I have been so endowed that I can put to sea another fleet as great as this we have lost whenever I choose. It does not matter if a stream is sometimes choked as long as the source flows freely." In fact, he was to make two more attempts to send an armada against England; each time, the ships were dispersed by storms.

The chief effect of the defeat of the armada of 1588 was psychological. Spain, whose *tercios,* or infantry troops, still maintained their aura of invincibility, continued to be a great power and a dangerous enemy but the nation's high point of prestige had passed.

Philip lived for ten years after that dark summer of 1588. He continued to labor over the paperwork of empire, falling farther and farther behind each year. He became more engrossed in religion, more distrustful, and more solitary. A Venetian ambassador described him at this time:

In earlier years he let himself be seen by the people once or twice a year in the corridor between his apartments and the chapel, but now he lives in seclusion. . . . He likes solitude and deserted places. He much enjoys the monastery of San Lorenzo de El Escorial, where he lives for long periods and constantly makes important additions to this sumptuous edifice. . . .

Philip's daughter the Infanta Isabella Clara Eugenia remained unwed until she was well over thirty. She

Two years after the armada's ignominious defeat, an unknown Flemish artist offered this allegorical interpretation of the tense political climate that prevailed in Europe. In his view, the "cow of the Netherlands" is goaded by Philip, fed by both Elizabeth I and William the Silent of Orange, and milked dry by the Duke of Alba, governor of the Spanish Netherlands. The sorely beset creature seems to share Elizabeth's disdain for the foppish Duke of Anjou (far left), one of the English queen's rejected French suitors.

was the light of her father's life, the only person he loved and had faith in. Her apartments at the Escorial adjoined his, and those simple quarters may be seen today just as they were when the princess was in residence. In the year of his death, Philip arranged his daughter's betrothal to her cousin Archduke Albert of Austria. Together they became sovereign rulers of the Netherlands, Philip giving up the Spanish claim to that country in a conciliatory move aimed at bringing about a Dutch peace.

In June 1598, Philip made his last journey from Madrid to the Escorial and prepared to die. He was suffering from ulcerating sores on his legs that were so painful he could not bear to have them touched. It was fifty-three days before he died, and during that time the unwashed sores became gangrenous and swarmed with maggots. Over the next few centuries Protestant writers seized upon the Spanish king's long, tortured death as evidence of God's displeasure with him. The nineteenth-century British traveler Richard Ford made a typical judgment:

> He lay long, like Job, on a dunghill of his own filth, consumed for 53 days, like Herod, by self-engendered vermin. . . . He was haunted with doubts whether his bloody bigotry, the supposed *merit* of his life, was not after all a damning crime. His ambition over, a ray of common-sense taught him to feel that a Moloch persecution breathed little of the true spirit of Christianity.

Sigüenza preferred to have the world believe that Philip had died in peace and saintliness and he recorded that during the king's final summer he had many charities performed in his name. He supplied dowries to large numbers of orphan girls who could

Attending to the elaborate preparations for his own funeral "as if it had been for someone else," Philip ordered that his black velvet funerary vestments be embroidered with skulls and crossbones — a highly appropriate choice for a man who spent some twenty years erecting the edifice that was to be his tomb.

otherwise not have found husbands, and he succored indigent widows and other unfortunates. Following Christ's injunction to forgive his enemies he ordered that the widow of his treasonous secretary Antonio Pérez be released from prison, where she had languished for many years, and that her daughter be allowed to inherit her mother's estate. He sent money to build altars at various shrines and churches of Spain, made contributions to hospitals, and pardoned many condemned prisoners.

In August Philip asked the papal nuncio to bless and absolve him, and on the first of September, in the evening, he asked for and received the last rites of the Church. Prince Philip, the infanta, and several high-ranking noblemen and prelates were present, as was Fray Sigüenza. "It seemed to me," writes the good monk, "that, judging by the interest with which the sainted king heeded and responded to everything, that he was not suffering pain and that he eagerly looked forward to receiving the last Sacrament."

In fact, Philip was not as close to death as is usual when people receive extreme unction; he lived twelve more days and was fully conscious until the hour he breathed his last. After the last rites, he sent everyone away except the prince, to whom he said, "I wanted you to be present at this act so that you might see the manner in which all comes to an end." Prince Philip, now twenty years old, had always been a disappointment to his father, who is said to have lamented, "God who has given me so many kingdoms has denied me a son capable of ruling them."

According to a quaint Elizabethan account of the king's last days, when Philip felt himself failing, he said, "I commaunde you to call hither your prince, which shall be your future king; and fetch hither unto me my coffin that I shall be laide in, and place here, upon this little cupboard, a dead man's skull crowned with my imperial crowne." He then sent for a coffer:

[And] taking forth a pretious stone of an infinite value, caused it to be delivered to his daughter. . . . And then, turning him to the Prince, said, "Are you contented with this, that I give unto your sister?" Who answered, "Yea, Sir; although you gave her all that I have." This answere lyking the King very wel, he willed them to looke in the cofer for another paper; and, giving it to the Prince, he told him, that therein he should see the forme how to govern his kingdome. [In fact, Philip had been schooling his son in the art of government for a number of years.] Then they tooke out of the said cofer a whip with bloudie knots, which the King holding up, said "This bloud is mine owne, and yet not mine, but my father's, who is in Heaven, who made use of this kind of exercise."

According to Sigüenza's account, which is probably more accurate, Philip made a final farewell to his children and then turned his thoughts to the matter of his funeral. Some days earlier, he had sent a message to the monks who kept the key to the coffin of the Emperor Charles V, instructing them to open it and see how the body was shrouded, so that his own body might be shrouded in the same manner. The dying monarch's orders regarding his coffin were given in detail — "as if," Sigüenza marveled, "it had been for someone else." The coffin was to be made of timbers from a ship that had fought against heretics. (The cross on the high altar of the church had also been constructed of timbers

Wearing his habitual garb — high ruff, unadorned costume, and Order of the Golden Fleece (above) — Philip posed for Pantoja de la Cruz in 1598, the year of his death. Too enfeebled by late summer to rise from his bed, Europe's mightiest monarch followed the services conducted at the High Altar through a door (right) in his bedroom.

from this ship.) Those boards, which came from an East Indian tree called the Tree of Paradise, had lain discarded in Lisbon for more than twenty years before they came to the attention of the king and were sent, at considerable expense, to the Escorial.

Philip's will, which he reportedly took "from under his pillow" and caused to be read aloud just before he died, asked that 30,000 masses be said at the Escorial for his soul. His coffin was to be lined in white silk and covered in black cloth-of-gold embroidered with a cross of red satin:

> [It is to be carried] by eight of my chiefest servants, all in mourning-weedes, with burning torches in their handes. The archbishop shall follow the Nobles, and our universal Heir shall follow on the one side all in dewle [mourning]. . . . Before shall be borne the Archbishop's banner; then the crosse; the monkes and the clergie presentlie shall followe, all in mourning garments. . . .

At five o'clock in the morning on September 13, 1598, as dawn was breaking and the boys of the seminary were singing mass, Philip died. Until his last breath, he held in one hand the same crucifix held by his father on his deathbed. His failing gaze was fixed on a relic held before him. "He was in the seventy-second year of his life," writes Sigüenza, "having been born on the 21st of May in the year 1527. He took over the government of these kingdoms in the year 1556. He began to build this monastery on the 23rd of April of 1563. Having laid the last stone in the year 1584, in the month of September, he had the pleasure of it for exactly fourteen years — which is another particular mercy of Heaven."

VI

Last of the Spanish Habsburgs

The bells of Spain tolled for nine days after the death of Philip II — and rightly so, for never again would Spain have a king of such intellectual capacity and such total devotion to duty. As Philip had feared, his son and successor, Philip III, proved to be an ineffectual leader. "Alas," the dying monarch had said, "I am afraid they will govern him." *They* were the courtiers and advisers with whom the young ruler surrounded himself, and very soon after his accession one of these, the Duke of Lerma, did assert himself above the rest and became the royal *privado,* or favorite. In medieval Spain favorites had often attained great power, but never under the strong sovereignties of Ferdinand and Isabella, Charles V, or Philip II.

Philip III loved pleasure as his father never had, and he devoted most of his time to hunting, dancing, and the theater. At the same time he was religious in a superstitious, childish way, and he alternated his amusements with elaborate penances. The Duke of Lerma, who had scarcely more ability than his king, relied on favorites of his own, men who were little more than rogues bent on enriching themselves. While Lerma, his favorites, and their relatives amassed fortunes, the poverty and suffering of the people of Spain grew steadily worse. The currency was debased, trade languished, and the countryside swarmed with bandits and vagabonds. Many of the country's enterprising young men emigrated to New Spain. The result was a labor shortage — one that Philip exacerbated by expelling some 275,000 Moriscos from the peninsula between 1609 and 1614. It was an emotionally popular move, but once the Moriscos were gone they were genuinely and unexpectedly missed, for they had been hardwork-

ing farmers, laborers, and artisans and it was not easy to replace them.

Among the diplomatic achievements of Philip III's reign was the termination of Spain's war with England in 1603 and the signing of a truce with the Netherlands in 1609. This allowed the exhausted Spanish forces a temporary respite from the protracted warfare in the north and permitted them to turn their attention to more pacific endeavors. As a result, Philip's reign was a culturally distinguished one. Cervantes became famous, Lope de Vega and Tirso de Molina flourished, and Calderón de la Barca got his start. The king was also an art patron; he augmented his father's collections, and under his aegis Spain exerted considerable cultural influence in Europe.

Philip III associated the Escorial with the penitential side of his life, and during the early years of his reign he seldom went there. After 1606, he began to visit it regularly, however, contributing jewels and sacred bones to the relic collection and four thousand splendid Arab, Turkish, and Persian manuscripts to the library. His queen, Margaret of Austria, died during childbirth at the Escorial in 1611. (One of their five children was Anne of Austria, who became the wife of Louis XIII and the mother of Louis XIV.) Philip personally superintended her funeral and burial, and from that time on his acts of piety increased. He often sought religious consolation from the prior of San Lorenzo el Real, and when he decided to dismiss the Duke of Lerma in 1617, the prior acted as his intermediary. That same year Philip began to plan a pantheon, or burial crypt, for the royal dead — a task bequeathed him by his father, who had said, "I have made a habitation for God only, and my son, if he wishes, may make one for my bones and the bones of my forefathers." However, when Philip's workmen set about enlarging the existing burial chamber they struck an underground spring that no one was able to control, and by the time the king died in 1621 construction work had virtually ceased.

Toward the end of his life Philip used to spend hours in the dank, uncompleted pantheon, hearing mass from the niche where he would someday be entombed, and sometimes lying down in it. He was only forty-one when he died — the result, it was said, of his having become overheated by sitting too close to a brazier. The French ambassador, Bassompierre, wrote that according to Spanish court etiquette braziers could only be moved by certain specified gentlemen, and that the day the king became overheated those gentlemen happened to be absent. The story is unquestionably apocryphal, although it is true that Spanish protocol was the most rigid in Europe. In actuality, Philip succumbed to erysipelas, also known as Saint Anthony's fire, an acute infectious disease of the skin and mucous membranes caused by a streptococcus bacterium and accompanied by inflammation, chills, and fever as well as by a change in the color of the skin to deep red. It is said that on his deathbed Philip made a vow to reform if the heavens saw fit to prolong his life. He died clutching the same crucifix that his father and grandfather had held when they died.

Philip IV was sixteen years old when he ascended the Spanish throne. He had recently been married to a lively French princess, Isabella of Bourbon, and both took much more interest in balls and festivals than in affairs of state. These Philip turned over to Spain's highly corrupt and virtually autonomous bureaucracy, a smoothly functioning political machine manned by such capable and ambitious ministers as Gaspar de Guzmán, the Count-Duke of Olivares. Olivares, a more honest and able administrator than the Duke of Lerma, struggled manfully for two crucial decades to extricate Spain from its fiscal and social morass. In the end, Philip's chief minister failed to restore the Spanish empire to its former glory, but he did almost singlehandedly halt the nation's spiraling decline during the first decades of the seventeenth century.

As Olivares's influence over the indolent and incompetent Philip IV grew, so did the prime minister's arrogance and power. The result was a series of domestic achievements — such as the laws he enacted to curb royal spending by prohibiting lavish dress and riotous living — accompanied by a series of foreign disasters. In 1621, for example, Olivares deliberately violated the Twelve Years' Truce with the Netherlands, a move that resulted in Spain's eventual expulsion from the Low Countries. And in 1636 he pitted Philip's troops against the French in the last phase of the Thirty Years' War. Spain's involvement in that inconclusive and enervating struggle ultimately forced Olivares to levy repressive new taxes in the king's name, and by 1643 Catalonia and Portugal were in open rebellion against the crown. To quell the rebels and restore civil order, Philip was obliged to exile his once-preeminent minister, who died two years later.

The commendable program of domestic reforms that Olivares embarked upon in his first year in office had just begun to take effect when a surprising emergency

in the spring of 1623 plunged Madrid into an orgy of extravagance. Charles Stuart, Prince of Wales — the future Charles I of England — suddenly presented himself in Madrid, having traveled across France and Castile incognito accompanied only by his father's favorite, the Duke of Buckingham. The purpose of his visit was to court the king's sister the Infanta Maria. As a contemporary English account put it:

> His princely desires serving him as wings to flye over the dangers of the Seas into Spain [so that] there might from their mutual enterviewes one of another a heavenly fire of Love be kindled, out of which might shine a memorable glory to both the Nations.

The prince, blond and handsome, was twenty-three; the infanta, rather pretty despite her Habsburg lip, was seventeen. Although the doyens of Spanish etiquette were horrified by Charles's unannounced arrival, the general public was delighted by such a romantic and unprecedented gesture, and every social class in Madrid began to celebrate. Austerity laws were forgotten in a pandemonium of fiestas, banquets, bullfights, and illuminations, and the streets resounded with a new popular song that began:

> Carlos Estuardo am I
> By love brought from afar.
> To the skies of Spain I come
> To see Maria, my star.

From the beginning it should have been clear to all concerned that marriage was out of the question. The granddaughter of Philip II, of course, could never become a Protestant, and although Charles was willing to make concessions — such as the right of Maria to oversee their children's education and the granting of

Only twenty-three when he moved to Madrid, Diego Velázquez served for three full decades as the foremost portraitist at the Spanish court. Like Sánchez Coello before him, Velázquez produced likenesses of virtually every member of the royal family; the haunting work at left, which is known as Las Meninas, *or* The Maids of Honor, *is among the most famous of those studies — and clearly one of the most complex. The Infanta Doña Margarita, who stands in a pool of suffused light at the center of the painting, is attended by two obsequious ladies-in-waiting and two dwarfs (lower right). In a sense, this canvas is also an essay on art, for in addition to the numerous identifiable paintings lining the walls, Velázquez has included himself in the composition. The mustachioed artist, visible at the far left, is working on a portrait of Philip IV and his queen, Mariana of Austria, whose images are reflected in the mirror above the infanta's head. Velázquez also added a self-portrait (far right) to the huge canvas above. The ten-by-twelve-foot* Surrender of Breda *re-creates the capitulation of that Dutch fortress-city on June 5, 1625. For Philip's commander, Ambrogio di Spinola — whom Velázquez has chosen to depict in gleaming black armor and a full sash — the victory at Breda capped a quarter of a century of military triumphs over the Dutch rebels.*

walls). He also found a simple way to put in a window and to build a staircase — "decent, spacious, majestic, and solemn" — so that funeral parties might easily enter the subterranean chamber.

Fray Nicolás completed his work in less than a year, but the redesigning and adorning of the pantheon with gilded chandeliers, marbles, bronzes, and the rest took nearly eight years more. At last, in March 1654 — almost a hundred years after Philip II had conceived of the Escorial itself at the battle of Saint-Quentin — the bodies of Charles V, Philip II, Philip III, and the queens who had been their mothers were brought to their permanent resting-place. Fray Nicolás was made a bishop, and there were new funeral obsequies. "Dry bones," intoned the monk who preached on the day of burial, "today you shall hear a sermon!"

The Pantheon of the Kings still looks very much as it did in 1654, a fittingly gloomy and splendid repository for royal coffins. Philip II would have approved the gloom, but the style of decoration, the first phase of Spanish baroque, would have bewildered him. Charles V would have been satisfied as to the disposition of his remains, which, in accordance with his wishes, lie directly beneath the feet of the priest who celebrates high mass in the church above. But he would have been displeased when Philip IV opened his coffin and had his body shown to the public. After ninety-six years, it was almost intact. According to a witness:

> The face well formed, the eyes whole, the chest strong and full, showing his invincible bravery and valiant heart, the arms as strong as them in the defense and preservation of the true Catholic faith, and all the other members so free from corruption that even the

digits of the hands and feet were preserved; only the nose was a trifle wanting.

At Yuste the coffin had been filled with heaps of wild rosemary and thyme, which were thought to have acted as a preservative. Philip IV believed otherwise: he wrote that Charles's body had been preserved because "the Lord has repaid him for his efforts in favor of the faith whilst he lived."

Philip's last few years were sober and depressing. He was trying to govern Spain himself, but in vain. During this period he corresponded with Sor Maria Coronel, a nun who not only influenced him to lead a less sinful life but gave him sound political advice as well. But it was too late for him to be an effective king. Spain had gained nothing through its costly involvement in the Thirty Years' War, and during the 1640's it had lost Portugal and only barely managed to keep the rebellious province of Catalonia in line. In 1659 Spain signed the Treaty of the Pyrenees with France, giving up various border states that had been Spanish since the days of Ferdinand and Isabella. Although the territorial losses were moderate, it was clear to the world that France, not Spain, was now the leading power in Europe. Under the treaty, Philip's elder daughter, Maria Theresa, became the wife of young Louis XIV. A large dowry was promised but never paid.

Philip became disconsolate and melancholy. He confessed to Sor Maria that he had once spent two hours kneeling in tears before the niche intended for his own coffin. In September 1665, at the Alcazar in Madrid, Philip fell mortally ill and resigned himself to death. When his courtiers asked him if they should bring the body of Saint Isidore to his bed in the hope of a cure,

he replied wearily that the corpse could intercede for him where it was, if it chose. He ordered 100,000 masses to be said at the Escorial for his soul, adding that any that were superfluous could assist other relatives "who might not yet have reached heaven."

In the wake of Philip IV's death there was such an indecent scramble for power among the nobles that they had to be reminded of their duty to accompany the funeral cortege to the Escorial. The wife of the English ambassador, Lady Fanshawe, and the rest of the diplomatic corps made the journey, and she tells us that the bier, suspended between two mules, was covered with cloth of gold and hung with crystal lanterns at each corner. Many grandees' coaches and a throng of noblemen on horseback followed, and the slow procession reached the Escorial during the night. Monks with lighted tapers came to the door of the church, and the prior asked the question prescribed by ritual: "Who is in that coffin?" The answer was, "It is the body of Philip the Fourth of Spain, whom we here bring for you to lay in his own tomb." After the burial, the mounted noblemen galloped back to Madrid with unseemly haste.

If some of these nobles were concerned for their country rather than for themselves, their haste was forgivable, for few countries have ever been in greater need of help. The new king, Charles II, was only four years old and so underdeveloped and sickly in body and mind that he was expected to die momentarily. He reigned for thirty-five years, however, a tragic victim of the repeated intermarriages of the Habsburgs. Not the least of his troubles was that he had inherited the family's protruding jaw in such an exaggerated

form that his teeth did not meet and he was forced to swallow his food unchewed, causing continual distress to his digestive system.

During his minority, no attempt was made to educate Charles for fear of overtaxing his feeble faculties. His incompetent mother, Mariana, attempted to act as regent, but she shortly turned for assistance to a young military captain named Fernando de Valenzuela, who became her favorite — and perhaps her lover. In his climb to power, Valenzuela ultimately found his path blocked by Don Juan José of Austria, a natural son of Philip IV, who was attempting to make himself regent in place of the queen. In 1678, Don Juan José temporarily succeeded in deposing Mariana. The queen fled Madrid, and Charles begged the monks at the Escorial to give sanctuary to Valenzuela.

Adherents of Don Juan José — including such important noblemen as the Duke of Medina-Sidonia and Don Antonio, eldest son of the Duke of Alba — tracked Valenzuela to the monastery and, after a heated interview with him arranged by the prior, determined to seize him. The monks concealed the queen's favorite in a secret cell while soldiers tramped all over the cloisters trying to find him. In high indignation, the prior thereupon excommunicated the Duke, Don Antonio, and the rest of the party. The bells and the organ were silenced, the monks ceased their chanting, and the candles of the church were extinguished until the intruders departed.

What followed reads like an adventure novel — and, in fact, the story of Valenzuela is said to have inspired Victor Hugo's *Ruy Blas*. The pursuers searched in vain for four days, often passing and repassing Valenzuela's

hiding place. They might never have found him if he had remained hidden, but hearing some soldiers near at hand, the young captain concluded that he was about to be discovered. He made a rope of knotted sheets and let himself out a window onto a slate roof, and thence into an attic of the church. From there he descended into the main cloister, where he came face to face with a sentry. He froze with fear, but the soldier decided to take pity on him and gave him the password.

After wandering aimlessly around the monastery, perhaps in a state of shock, Valenzuela came upon the dormitory of the novitiates; he pounded on their door and begged them to save him. The young men were anxious to do so, but they were new to the monastery and knew no secure hiding places. All forty of them left their dormitory, and with Valenzuela concealed in their midst, they went en masse to the library and hid him into a storage attic, placing a picture over the entrance. Their unusual activity was reported to Don Antonio, who arrived the next morning and took the fugitive prisoner. After a lengthy imprisonment and the loss of the estates conferred upon him by Mariana, Valenzuela was banished to the Philippines. Later he was permitted to go to Mexico, where he died in 1692.

Meanwhile, those who had been excommunicated petitioned the prior for pardon. In no hurry to comply, the prior referred the matter to the pope, who eventually lifted the ban. Don Juan José lost popular favor not long afterward, and the queen mother resumed the regency and continued to tilt for power until her death in 1696.

In 1671, while Charles was still a child, there was a devastating fire at the Escorial. It started in a chimney, and burned for five days, destroying priceless books and paintings as well as roofs, walls, and furniture. When it was finally extinguished, the queen mother issued an edict ordering persons within an area of six leagues to assist in clearing away the rubble and debris. And as the king grew up his feeble mind was gripped by the idea of restoring his great-grandfather's sprawling granite monument.

In the sacristy, which had been badly damaged, Charles founded the Altar of the Miraculous Host in honor of a sacred wafer acquired by Philip II during the last decade of his life. The wafer had been trampled underfoot by heretic soldiers in the Netherlands, and blood was said to have exuded from the marks made by their hobnail boots. Twice a year that sacred wafer is exhibited to the faithful; at all other times it is concealed behind a magnificent altarpiece, designed by the Spanish artist Claudio Coello, that shows Charles II and his court adoring the Miraculous Host. The courtiers' painted portraits speak eloquently of the atmosphere that surrounded the hapless, empty-headed king, who is shown holding his candle awry. Only the face of the prior is wise and sensitive. The others suggest simplicity, superstitious awe, indifference, cynicism, ignorance, and — in the face directly behind the king — something approaching evil.

Coello, who was the last great Spanish painter of the seventeenth century, is said to have died of disgust when he heard that the Neapolitan Luca Giordano had been commissioned to execute a series of frescoes in the church and above the great staircase of the Escorial. No frescoes had been added to San Lorenzo el Real since the death of Luca Cambiaso, a hundred years be-

fore, and there were vast stretches of unadorned ceiling. Giordano was widely known and admired for his facility at painting soaring heavens filled with free-floating angels, for his lively color — and, above all, for his amazingly speedy execution, which had earned him the nickname "Luca Fa Presto," Luke Make Haste.

During the autumn, winter, and early spring of 1694–95, Giordano contributed seven large frescoes to the church and cloister at the Escorial. Charles was deeply interested in the Neapolitan's progress, and he urged the prior to give the artist every comfort and attention. Messengers went back and forth each week between the court and the monastery, carrying detailed reports and queries concerning the progress of the frescoes. The king sent instructions concerning the most minor details, and he often came in person to view the work. As Philip IV had been able to forget his cares on visits to the studio of Velázquez, so his troubled son, Charles II, found relief in watching the rapid brush of Luca Giordano, who was the most noteworthy of the foreign painters to work at the Escorial during the seventeenth century. In the course of a highly productive decade that began in 1692, the talented Neapolitan executed a number of commissions at the Escorial. In addition, he was called upon to decorate the Salón de Embajadores, or Ambassadors' Corridor, at the royal palace in Madrid, as well as the Cathedral of Toledo. Giordano remained in Spain until after Charles's death in 1700, and he returned to Naples a rich man.

At the joyless court of the "bewitched" king, Giordano must have been one of the few happy and contented figures. Charles's first queen was the French princess Marie Louise of Orleans, a charming girl who had been brought up in the gay and sophisticated court of her uncle Louis XIV — and who was, consequently, appalled by the stiff ceremony of the Spanish court. Her French attendants were sent away and so were her French clothes — and even the caged talking birds she had brought with her (because the birds spoke in French) were removed. The seemingly irrepressible queen persisted in riding horseback, however, even though Spanish ladies considered it indecent because it allowed the feet to be seen. "A Spanish lady," wrote Madame d'Aulnoy, a gossipy memoirist of the day, "after she has granted the last favor to her lover, will shew him her feet." Since it was impermissible for a groom to touch a queen, Marie Louise had to mount and dismount unassisted.

Spanish royalty performed its daily rounds on an immutable schedule. The queen's bedtime was ten in the summer and nine in winter, and "it frequently happened as she was eating her supper some of her women, without saying a word to her, would begin to undress her head and others to pull off her shoes under the table and so hurry her to bed."

Charles was very fond of his pretty French wife. After putting in about a quarter of an hour each day on affairs of state, he spent the rest of his time in childish games in which Marie Louise patiently joined him. Sometimes he would pick strawberries in the garden and then sit counting and recounting them. Or, as one of his ministers records, he would run back and forth through the palace "like a child of six . . . and his conversation would match about the same age."

No children resulted from the royal marriage, and Marie Louise was blamed. (She wrote secretly to

France to report that the king was incapable of fathering a child.) In 1689, the unhappy girl died, and soon thereafter she was succeeded by a German princess, Maria Anna of Bavaria-Neuburg. Maria Anna lacked the charm of her predecessor and she refused to join Charles in romping or in counting strawberries. In fact, she frightened him. It soon became clear that there would be no issue to this marriage either, and an international storm over the Spanish succession arose. The new queen seems to have seen herself as some sort of high-level secret agent, working in behalf of a Habsburg archduke who happened to be her brother-in-law. She nagged Charles about her scheme continually, but others importuned him with the merits of one of the Bavarian princes and of Philip, Duke of Anjou, grandson of Louis XIV and his Spanish queen, Maria Theresa (see genealogy, page 164).

During the last few years of his reign, Charles was in continual pain from his various physical defects and in mental anguish over the matter of the succession. He went often to the Escorial, happier among the kind and simple monks than among the base and superstitious intriguers who surged around him at court. Fanatics, abetted by the queen, claimed that they could exorcise the devil that had bewitched Charles, and they continually troubled him with magic spells and potions. Someone convinced him that seeing the bodies of his dead ancestors would prompt the spirits of those personages to pray in heaven for his good health, and one day he and Maria Anna descended into the pantheon and had several coffins opened. "The Queen Mother . . . was as entire as the first day and without the least offence," noted a contemporary. "The Queen carried the expression of her filial respect beyond what I had ever heard of before by taking her hand and kissing it. Another body, I think it was that of Philip the Third, seemed entire, but when they touched it, fell in pieces." When the coffin of Charles's first wife, the hapless Marie Louise, was opened, he wept copiously, kissing and caressing the body until he fell into a fit.

This unusual brand of medical therapy failed to take effect. "The king is so very weak, he can scarcely lift his hand to his head to feed himself," an observer at court reported in 1698, adding that Charles was so melancholy that neither his buffoons, dwarfs, nor puppet-shows could in the least divert him from the notion that everything that was said or done to him was a temptation of the devil. Never thinking himself safe except with his confessor and two friars by his side, Charles insisted that they join him in his chamber every night. Nevertheless, the observer noted, "the queen lugs him out abroad every day . . . though he looks like a ghost and moves like an image of clockwork. They talk of a diet of hens and capons fed with vipers' flesh."

At last, on November 1, 1700, the tragic king was able to die. Unmourned, he went to his dark marble tomb in the Escorial, while his last will and testament bequeathed the Spanish throne to Philip of Anjou.

Directly beneath the High
Altar of the basilica — and
thus at both the physical and
the spiritual heart of the
Escorial — lie the corpses of
eleven Spanish kings, among
them Charles V and the three
Philips who succeeded him.
Their gray marble coffins
(near right) are separated by
a low altar from the banked
coffins of their queens. Anna
of Austria, Philip II's fourth
wife, rests across from him in
the second tier; Isabella of
Bourbon, Philip IV's first wife,
occupies a corresponding
bottom niche. The pantheon's
polished marble surfaces are
accented with burnished bronze.

VII

In the Absence of Royalty

For more than half a century after Charles II's death the Escorial lay neglected by its royal owners. The new king, Philip V, with his French ways and tastes, felt no affinity for it, and he built a new palace, La Granja, across the mountains in the direction of Segovia. Since medieval times there had been a Hieronymite monastery and a royal hunting lodge on the site of La Granja, and Philip's first intention was to emulate his mighty ancestor and build an imposing church and monastery with a modest palace attached to it. However, Philip, founder of the Bourbon dynasty in Spain, was no austere puritanical Catholic; his childhood had been spent at the worldly and extravagant court of Louis XIV. (Louis himself may have had the Escorial in mind when he began building Versailles, but that palace had become a celebration not of God but of himself and France.) As a result, La Granja did not turn out to be a small version of the Escorial but a beautifully appointed royal palace to which a church and monastery — and the most magnificent formal gardens in all of Spain — were appended.

Spain was at war for all but six of Philip's forty-six years on the throne. The War of the Spanish Succession (1701–1714), fought by France and Spain to defend Philip's throne against an alliance of England, the Protestant Netherlands, Austria, Portugal, and the Holy Roman Empire, ended with Philip's keeping his crown but losing a great deal of Spanish territory. Gibraltar and Minorca were ceded to England; Milan, Naples, Sardinia, and the Spanish Netherlands (modern Belgium) to Austria; and Sicily to Savoy. Spain retained its New World colonies, but Philip was obliged to grant England certain commercial rights,

among them an *asiento,* or contract, for supplying slaves to Spain's New World holdings for a period of thirty years. Catalonia, which had rebelled once again, was subdued and deprived of its traditional civil rights, as was the rest of Spain. Philip yearned to reign absolutely, but instead he spent his life being ruled by others — first his grandfather Louis XIV and the French agents whom Louis sent to Spain to keep an eye on the young monarch; and later his second wife, Elizabeth Farnese, whose determination to find thrones for their numerous children brought Spain into continual conflict with Austria.

Philip V abdicated in 1724 in favor of his son Louis. The forty-one-year-old monarch said that he wanted to spend the rest of his life in religious seclusion, but many observers suspected that, driven by his wife, he was secretly hoping to succeed Louis XV of France, who was then in poor health and without an heir. But when young Louis of Spain died within the year, Philip resumed the crown — which he retained until he himself died in 1746. His last years, spent chiefly at La Granja, were marred by fits of melancholia; some said he was completely mad. He and Elizabeth Farnese, who survived him by twenty years, chose to be buried in the light and airy church at La Granja rather than in the black-and-bronze gloom of the Escorial's pantheon.

Philip's heir, Ferdinand VI, was a greater lover of peace than was his father, and throughout his thirteen-year reign he avoided war while attempting to bring about reforms within the country. But like his father, Ferdinand suffered from interludes of black depression during which he could do no work. The king's consort, Maria Magdalena Barbara of Portugal, with whom he was very much in love, had a horror of the Escorial. "We are going to keep company with dead kings and men in shrouds," she remarked on one occasion when she was obliged to go there. The royal couple avoided the grandiose mausoleum in life and escaped it in death: they were buried in Madrid.

The only historical event of any note that took place at the Escorial during these years was the gathering in 1733 of a large number of French and Spanish Bourbon families and their ministers to sign an agreement of solidarity known to historians as The First Family Compact or The Escorial Compact. This alliance of France and Spain was to be an important factor in European politics, linking the diplomatic fortunes of the two countries for nearly sixty years — until the French Bourbons were swept away by revolution.

In 1759 Ferdinand VI was succeeded by his half brother Charles, who came to the throne at the age of forty-three, having been ruler first of Parma and then of the Kingdom of the Two Sicilies for many years. Charles was accustomed to an urbane society, and unlike most Spaniards he was fully aware of the new theories of the Age of Reason. He was shocked to find Spain wallowing in a slough of backwardness and superstition akin to the one in which Charles II had left it at the beginning of the century. There were no good roads, and even Madrid lacked such elementary amenities as streetlights or a system of garbage collection. Education was dominated by a narrow-minded church, and the cloisters were crowded with ignorant and idle priests and nuns. Most of the work in the nation was done by foreigners because of the deep-seated Spanish notion that labor and good breeding were incompatible with high social standing.

Charles III, an absolute monarch, immediately began to dispense enlightenment with an autocratic hand. For example, madrileños who insisted on slouching around the streets of the capital wrapped in traditional long cloaks found themselves being taken into custody and having their long cloaks shortened by government-appointed tailors. Surprised by his subjects' loud objections, King Charles took the advice of one of his ministers and tried a more subtle, psychological approach. To discourage his subjects from wearing the long cloak, he made it the official uniform of the hangman. On a more important level, he curbed the power of the church and the Inquisition, and he put through much-needed economic and bureaucratic reforms. He even went so far as to issue a royal decree reassuring the Spanish gentry that performing manual labor would not automatically deprive them of their status as hidalgos, or minor noblemen.

Charles was very fond of hunting, and no doubt chiefly for that reason he took to frequenting the Escorial, where the surrounding mountains were still as bountiful a source of game as they had been in the days of Philip II. He liked to live simply, but his wife, a princess of Saxony who found Spain woefully provincial ("With Spanish ladies there is nothing whatever to talk about"), did not care to accompany him to the outmoded and rundown royal quarters at the Escorial.

In the course of his twenty-nine-year reign Charles made a number of improvements in the area, and he allowed the monks to build a tunnel from their monastery to the hamlet, to protect them from the frigid winter winds that sweep down from the Guadarramas.

He also introduced the monks to the principles of fire fighting. But it was his son and daughter-in-law, the nondescript and unfortunate Charles IV and the disreputable Maria Louisa of Parma, who made the Escorial a comfortable retreat for royalty, decorating room after room of the old palace in the style of the late eighteenth century. Today these rooms are resplendent with rich draperies, heavily gilded furniture, and intricately painted walls and ceilings — but all their grandeur pales and is forgotten beside the real treasure to be found there, five tapestries designed by the great Spanish master Goya.

Francisco José de Goya y Lucientes, born in 1746, first came to the attention of Charles IV as a designer at the royal tapestry factory of Santa Barbara. The original cartoons (as the designs are called) for the Escorial tapestries may be seen at the Prado. The tapestries themselves, with their brilliant scenes of Spanish peasant life, bring an almost out-of-keeping warmth and vigor to the Escorial's otherwise regally chill interiors. The visitor to Spain should stop first at the Prado to see not only the cartoons but also Goya's portraits of Charles IV and Queen Maria Louisa, their odious favorite Godoy (the king's prime minister and the queen's lover), and their hateful heir, Ferdinand. He then should take the tour of the rooms at the Escorial where all four ate, slept, plotted, and frittered away their time. The portrait of Maria Louisa on the horse Godoy gave her, now in the Prado, was painted at the Escorial.

The king had a suite of private rooms at the Escorial whose floors, doors, and shutters were all made of marquetry with delicate designs of flowers, ribbons,

*Francisco José de Goya y Lucientes's unflinchingly
accurate portrait of his patron Charles III (left)
shows the avuncular monarch leaning on a fowling
piece. Months after he appointed Goya to the post
of court painter, Charles died and his corpulent
son Charles IV ascended the throne. Goya's study of
the new king and his large family (above) reveals
the ostentation that typified the Spanish Bourbons.*

vases, and other classical motifs. It was in these rooms, in October 1807, that he found upon his dressing table an anonymous note of a very disturbing nature. "Haste, haste, haste!" it said, "Prince Ferdinand prepares a movement in the palace; the Crown is in peril; and Queen Maria Louisa runs great risk of death by poison. It is urgent not to lose an instant to impede the plot."

A series of political events that were beyond the understanding of this slow-witted monarch had led him to this predicament: Napoleon Bonaparte, who had been sweeping through all Europe, had recently turned his attention to the Iberian Peninsula. His immediate and avowed victim was Portugal, marked by him for conquest and partition because of its alliance with England. In reality, the French emperor was more concerned with sealing the serious breach that Iberia left in his vaunted Continental System, which had been devised to humble and weaken England through economic sanctions.

The year 1807 found Napoleon negotiating secretly with the unscrupulous Godoy to arrange for the passage of French troops through Spain on the way to overcome Portugal, one third of which he promised to Godoy as a personal principality. Ignorant of these plans, Prince Ferdinand had secretly approached the emperor through the French ambassador in Madrid. He wanted nothing less than Napoleon's backing in a scheme to overthrow the king and queen and their favorite Godoy, after which he would ascend the throne himself. Since Ferdinand's first wife had died the year before, he also begged the emperor "to deign to grant me a princess of his august house for a wife."

No one knows who left the note on King Charles's dressing table. In any event, Charles showed it to the queen and, summoning an armed guard, they hastened together along the echoing stone corridors to Ferdinand's apartments. They found him trying to conceal papers that were so compromising as to warrant his immediate arrest for high treason and contemplated parricide. He was locked up forthwith in the prior's cell, from which he is said to have communicated with friends with the aid of a fishing line.

Luckily for Ferdinand, Godoy decided that Spain would fare better vis-à-vis Napoleon if the royal family presented a united front. His wish was Maria Louisa's command, and she came to the rescue of the very son who had been about to have her poisoned. The weeping queen ultimately persuaded her husband to overlook Ferdinand's treasonous behavior on the condition that he would apologize to his parents. "The voice of nature disarms the hand of vengeance," Charles wrote in an open letter to his subjects — and turned the young delinquent loose.

But Charles and Maria Louisa had only a few more months on the throne. It soon became apparent that Napoleon had tricked both Godoy and Ferdinand, and that the 100,000 French troops in Spain were not an army in transit but an occupying force. The king and queen decided to flee to the Americas; they got as far as the royal palace of Aranjuez, south of Madrid, when word came that Godoy's palace in Madrid had been sacked and Godoy himself nearly killed. A furious mob converged on Aranjuez, demanding the head of Godoy. To save him, Charles abdicated in favor of Ferdinand, who promptly asked Napoleon to support his regime.

The emperor had other plans, however. He lured

both parents and son over the border into France for a "consultation." And after a stormy scene during which Charles struck his son and Maria Louisa screamed at him, the emperor had all three taken into custody. Charles abdicated in favor of Napoleon and spent the rest of his life in exile. Napoleon said of him, "Carlos is a good old man." But of the queen, he wrote, "Maria Louisa has her past and her character written on her face, which is all I need say. It surpasses anything one dare imagine." As for Ferdinand, he remarked after having spent some time with him, "He is very grasping, eats four times a day, and has no idea of anything." Ferdinand was detained as a state prisoner in France, living in idleness and vice on Talleyrand's estate until Napoleon's downfall in 1814.

During the years between 1808 and 1814 Spain was torn by a particularly bloody war, one in which the French and the minority of Spaniards who supported Joseph Bonaparte — who had been placed on the Spanish throne by his brother — combated a popular movement in favor of the undeserving Ferdinand. The word *guerrilla* was invented during this war as a term for the unorganized and undisciplined Spanish patriots who harassed the invaders wherever they turned. During the winter of 1812-13, while Napoleon was going down to defeat in Russia, English troops under Lord Wellington advanced across Spain and into France. In March 1814 the defeated emperor released Ferdinand, who resumed the Spanish throne. His powers were far from absolute, however, for in the years that Napoleon's brother Joseph had ruled *de jure,* a central junta had ruled *de facto* — and that junta had drafted and refined the famed Constitution of 1812. Adopted by the

Constituent Cortes (parliament) of Cadiz soon after Napoleon embarked on his disastrous Russian campaign, that landmark document introduced the principle of constitutional monarchy to Spain. At the same time it abolished the Inquisition and governmental censorship and terminated such archaic forms of bureaucratic graft as the sale of offices.

The Escorial suffered egregious harm during the six years that King Joseph sat on Spain's throne. In the spring of 1808, French officers were billeted in the monastery and troops were billeted in the seminary, and they were far from respectful of their surroundings. After the bloody fighting in Madrid between the Spanish populace and French troops — the subject of Goya's paired masterpieces *The Second of May* and *The Third of May* — the monks were peremptorily ordered to turn the monastery into a military hospital. Later, King Joseph Bonaparte allowed the Hieronymites to remain in the monastery but condoned a systematic looting of its greatest treasures. He ordered the entire library — 30,000 printed books and 4,300 manuscripts — to be moved to Madrid. After the French defeat the library was returned, but 10,000 volumes were found to be missing, among them the Index of Forbidden Books.

A shadowy figure named Frederic Quilliet is said to have organized the removal of the paintings and jewels. A year or two before the French occupation, he had spent some months at the Escorial posing as an innocent traveler and lover of religious art and relics, and during that time he had persuaded the unsuspecting monks to show him all their treasures. Quilliet returned in 1808 with the French army and directed

the removal of the most desirable paintings and the most valuable jeweled reliquaries, from which the sacred bones were removed and impiously tossed back to the monks.

One of the most valuable of these reliquaries was a silver statue showing Saint Lawrence holding one of the grids upon which he was martyred. The iron grid, torn from its splendid gold setting, is still in the relic collection, but both the statue and the setting were included in one of the three hundred cartloads of treasures taken away by the French. The Miraculous Host, in its magnificent reliquary, was hidden in a door lintel and sealed in with mortar by one of the monks. But the Cellini Christ was removed, and at the same time the interior tabernacle of the high altar disappeared forever.

Fortunately for the Escorial, Quilliet had no taste for Velázquez and took none of the master's priceless canvases. But fifty paintings, including several by Goya, were especially earmarked for Napoleon; after the emperor's downfall they were found in Paris in a big, unlabeled wooden cylinder. Although the monks were unable to prevent the removal of the paintings, they did succeed in getting Joseph Bonaparte to countermand Quilliet's order that the monastery bells be smelted down into cannon.

In the summer of 1812, the advancing British and Portuguese armies occupied the Escorial. Cannon were set up in the orchards and shoemakers worked in the library during those weeks. After the death from fever of an English major-general, Lord Wellington stopped by and ordered an inscribed stone for the officer's grave in the monastery garden. In December,

the French returned, and with them came Marshal
Soult, an avid — and consequently disappointed — art
collector who could find nothing left to take.

One of the few useful accomplishments of King
Ferdinand VII following his return from Paris in 1814
was a thorough restoration of the Escorial. He had
been born there, and it seems to have been one of his
favorite palaces. As a young man he had lived at the
great monastery-palace for long periods of time, perhaps in order to get away from his parents and Godoy.
Ferdinand chose to spend his honeymoon with his first
wife at the Escorial, and when the king died in 1833
the grateful monks accorded him an exact duplicate of
Philip II's funeral. The Hieronymites were among
Ferdinand's few admirers, and he earned himself the
reputation of "the worst king Spain ever had." He was
despotic, vindictive, vicious, two-faced, stupid, childish,
dissolute, and cowardly. In addition, he was an un-
usually ugly man; besides a drooping nose, he had a
pronounced Habsburg lip, and in his later years he became bloated and fat.

Ferdinand was childless until the last few years of his
life, when his niece and fourth consort, Maria Cristina
of Naples, presented him with two daughters. For more
than a hundred years, there had been a law in Spain
against the crown descending through the female line;
legally, therefore, the succession should have passed to
Ferdinand's younger brother, Carlos. But on his deathbed Ferdinand changed the law and named his two-
year-old daughter, Isabella, as queen and her mother
as regent. This arrangement could not have been worse
for Spain, for it plunged the country once more into a
civil war — between the Carlists (those who supported

Carlos) and those who supported Isabella. The queen-regent, still a flighty young girl, neglected her official duties for a secret love affair and marriage with a corporal in her bodyguard.

Little Queen Isabella grew up to be as spoiled and willful as her father, although she had a more agreeable personality. At thirteen she was declared of age; by that time the great powers of Europe were taking a lively interest in the choice of a husband for her. Queen Victoria favored a prince of the House of Coburg; Louis Philippe of France wanted a Bourbon, although the English made it very clear to him that they would not countenance the choice of one of his own sons, for that would bind France and Spain too closely. The queen-regent advanced the name of her own brother, a prince of Naples; and many Spaniards fervently hoped that the Carlist pretender would settle for the role of king-consort and put an end to the civil war.

This international intriguing went on for three years and seems to have taken into consideration everything except the young queen's happiness. At last, in October 1846, Isabella was married at the Escorial to a Bourbon cousin, Francisco de Asís; and at the same time her fourteen-year-old sister was married to the Duke of Montpensier, a son of Louis Philippe. It was a splendid occasion but scarcely a happy one, for the queen's bridegroom was a homosexual, and the union, based only on political expediency, had little chance of success. The King of France apparently hoped that Isabella would be childless and that one of her sister's children would inherit the throne. But, as a French observer remarked, ". . . the queen has plenty of faithful subjects who can replace [Francisco] in case of need"

— and apparently this is precisely what happened. Although the queen and her consort lived in separate wings of the palace she produced one child after another, confounding Louis Philippe and shocking that other young queen, Victoria.

At the Escorial, Isabella planned and began the construction of the Pantheon of the Infantes — a burial place for the bodies of queens who were not the mothers of kings, as well as for royal children and one distinguished royal bastard, Don Juan of Austria. There are nine sepulchral chambers in the pantheon, none of aesthetic merit unless one is an admirer of blinding displays of white Italian marble. The "mausoleum of the infantes" is a triumph of bad taste — a twenty-sided white marble object, tiered like a wedding cake and containing sixty recesses in which the coffins of children of assorted sizes are stacked and filed away as if they were office records.

A description of an infanta's funeral was written in the last century by Frances Erskine Inglis Calderón de la Barca, the Scottish wife of a Spanish diplomat. Because of her husband's position, Señora Calderón chose to publish the story of her Madrid experiences under the pretense that they were written by a German attaché. However, her sharp eye for detail is very feminine and her dispassionate view of the long-drawn-out ceremonies she witnessed at the Escorial is typical of a forthright Scot.

"Three days have elapsed since my visit to the Escorial, and I have not yet thawed," she begins. "All was on a gigantic scale; the ceremonies, the building, the cold. The coldness of the day, one of the most severe we have had in Madrid, was almost unbearable

Goya's first task at the Spanish court involved designing the cartoons, or preliminary paintings, from which the tapestries used to decorate the royal palaces were woven. He worked unassisted on the originals, such as the study of al fresco dancers at left; teams of skilled weavers then faithfully reproduced his oil studies as tapestries. Some of these artistic collaborations, among them The Kite *(right), hang in the Bourbon Palace of the Escorial.*

within the precincts of the Escorial, but it was a scene which I can never forget." For two days the body of the three-day-old princess had been lying in state in the royal chapel of the palace at Madrid on a bed hung with yellow satin that was embroidered with raised work of silver. On the evening of the second day, the body had been placed in a glass-topped lead casket, which in turn was put into a second one lined with silver tissue and gold lace. Under a pall of cloth-of-gold, it was put into a hearse "of massive mahogany, all adorned with branches and garlands of artificial flowers, and hangings of white satin, with embroidery and borders, arrows, cords and tassels of gold."

At eight o'clock the following morning, the funeral procession set out for the Escorial. The entourage included monks and psalmists of the royal chapel, lords of the royal household, several high-ranking prelates, cavalry, trumpeters, and part of the queen's guard followed by the carriages of the diplomatic corps. Because of lengthy delays at the many villages they passed through, it was dusk long before the procession reached the Escorial:

I strained my eyes in the darkness to distinguish this wonderful monument. . . . It loomed out in the darkness, immense, mysterious, lonely. The snowy crowns of the Guadarramas were distinctly visible. The wind blew fiercely, and sounded like a sad and moaning requiem, proceeding from the everlasting hills. The stars shone out clearly and coldly, through the dark clouds that were blown across their silvery disks.

The cortege came to a halt before the main gate, where a bier had been prepared to receive the coffin and a long procession of chaplains and churchmen,

headed by the abbot in his cope, advanced to meet the body. After an exchange of ritual phrases having to do with the identification of the body, holy water was thrown over it and the air swelled with the chanting of the monks:

It seemed as if all the winds of heaven were unchained that night, their hoarse voices howling round the massive building, blowing through the vaults, extinguishing the great torches, and moaning in tones that sounded like the wailing of infernal spirits or of souls in agony. . . . "A hut for myself, a palace for God," said the monarch who designed this glorious pile. I cannot pretend to describe it, for all was indistinct in gloom and grandeur. The blazing lights which yet but faintly illuminated the immense cathedral — the echo of the music, *Beati immaculati in via* — the abbots and priests — grandees and officers in uniform — all this preparation for receiving the remains of an infant who had scarcely opened her eyes on the light.

After the funeral service the guests were ushered into a tapestried hall where an enormous fire burned and a feast awaited them. After dining they were shown to their sleeping quarters, and the following morning the official mourners reassembled in the church for a pontifical mass. Then, with more ceremonious exchanges of phrases, the exterior coffin was locked and the entire party moved down the stairs into the royal pantheon (the Pantheon of the Infantes had not yet been built), where the coffin was placed on a bier in the center of the chamber:

At the same moment a discharge of musketry was fired by the garrison. We reascended the gloomy staircase leading from the sepulchre. The iron doors were

closed and the little princess was left to moulder into dust amongst her royal ancestors. The absurd fancy that she must suffer from the coldness and gloom to which she was abandoned haunted me for hours afterward. . . . As we drove off, I took one last look at the Escorial, now brilliantly illuminated by the morning sun! Alone in a desert, it can be compared with no surrounding object, unless with the lofty mountains behind it.

Both Maria Cristina and Isabella were thorough believers in absolutism and made every effort to prevent Spain from obtaining parliamentary government. In 1868, seething discontent finally erupted in open revolution, the first ever directed against the dynasty, and Isabella fled into exile. The leaders of the revolution, basically rather conservative, believed that Spain should have a king, if a democratic one could be found. In 1871, after looking all over Europe, they finally offered the throne to Amadeo, a son of Victor Emmanuel II of Italy. He was a man of good will but no great capability and finding the job much too difficult he stepped down in 1873. Two years later, after a great deal of confusion and turmoil, the military leaders who were ruling the country invited Isabella's seventeen-year-old son to assume the Spanish throne as Alfonso XII (see genealogy, page 164).

Spain continued to be badly governed, despite creditable efforts by Alfonso. He died six months before the birth of his heir, Alfonso XIII, who was therefore king from the moment of his birth in 1886 until he went into exile in 1931 — although during his minority his mother, a Habsburg princess, acted as regent.

The events that led up to Alfonso XIII's departure are too complicated to set down in a brief space, nor do they have anything to do with the Escorial. Alfonso left Spain alone, but by a quirk of fate his consort and their children, on their way into exile, boarded their train at Escorial in order to avoid the hostile crowds gathered in Madrid. The queen, a granddaughter of Queen Victoria, received the last homage of her ladies and of about a hundred loyal Spaniards while sitting by the roadside in the village of Escorial, waiting for the royal train that was to carry her and the children to safety in France.

The story of the Escorial is all but told. During the Spanish Civil War of the 1930's, it suffered minor damage and losses, but it was only recently that a danger to its very existence was discovered, working silently within its granite walls. Termites, billions of them, were destroying the great timbers of the roofs and towers, as well as the mortar that held the stones together. Some of the towers were already tipping. Unchecked, the tiny insects would have accomplished what fires and wars had failed to do. However, their onslaught was halted in time; during the 1960's the Spanish government carried out an extensive and costly restoration of the palace, church, and monastery.

The monastery is now in the hands of a community of Augustinians — the Hieronymites were expelled from Spain during the 1830's when many monkish orders were banned and their monasteries were seized. The palace and picture gallery are administered by the very efficient Patrimonio Nacional, which maintains the complex for the benefit of tourists.

The "eighth wonder of the world" has always been a tourist attraction, ever since that day in 1584 when

Philip II sent the visiting Japanese delegates in carriages to see it. Its early visitors usually declared themselves to be awestruck and overcome; when a certain Captain Carleton saw the Escorial in 1712, he reacted in typical fashion: "I feasted my eyes with extraordinaries which would have justified a twelvemonth's journey on purpose. The structure is entirely magnificent, beyond any thing I ever saw or anything my imagination could frame." As a timid word of criticism, he added, "I have seen many other parts of Spain where that glorious building would have shone with yet far greater splendor."

The Duke of Saint-Simon spent three days at the Escorial in 1721 and found the monks "rude and superstitious," although he admired their pharmacy and gardens. "The Pantheon frightened me with its horror and majesty," he noted. "The high altar and the sacristy made my eyes pop with their immense richness." And Voltaire himself remarked of Philip II that the Spanish monarch had apparently supposed that "God could be bought with buildings."

French writers of the romantic age made Spain a special point of pilgrimage — lured, perhaps, by stories brought home by Napoleonic soldiers. As they did not share the Catholic zeal of earlier generations, what struck them most forcibly was its atmosphere of death and gloom. A particularly vivid description was given by François René de Chateaubriand, the French writer and statesman who visited Spain about 1808:

The Escorial showed me, with only one rite and only one monument, the bleakness of Castile. . . . It contained filled and partially filled tombs; a library in which spiders had left their marks, and the master-pieces of Raphael, blackened in an empty sacristy. Its 1,140 windows, about three-quarters of them broken, opened to the wide spaces of heaven and earth. . . . Around the formidable monastery was a park grown over with broom. This Versailles of the steppes had inhabitants only during the reign of kings. I saw the redwing, the lark of the heather, poised on the roof. . . . Nothing was more imposing than this dark and saintly architecture, with its invincible belief, with its grace, with its taciturn experience. . . . Through these funeral constructions the shadow of the man in black could be seen passing: Philip, its builder.

Théophile Gautier was perhaps the harshest of these nineteenth-century French observers:

I came away from this desert of granite, this monkish necropolis, with an extraordinary sensation of satisfaction and relief. . . . I was delivered from that architectural nightmare which I had thought would never end. I advise those persons who have the idiocy to maintain that they are bored to go and pass three or four days at the Escorial; there they will discover what real tedium means, and find amusement for the rest of their lives in the thought that they might be in the Escorial, but are not.

Gautier's unconcealed disdain for Philip's "monkish necropolis" must be balanced against the more even-handed and dispassionate views of twentieth-century visitors, most of whom have viewed the Escorial as a near-perfect reflection of Philip II's imperfect conception of God's dwelling place on earth. Far from being disappointed by the monument's monotonous façade, recent visitors have been impressed by the quintessentially Spanish nature of the mammoth monastery-

Nothing more perfectly expresses the spiritual essence of the Escorial than this highly elaborate eighteenth-century allegory, Philip V, Conqueror of Heresy. *It pictures the king and blind Faith (left) as well as the queen and her young son (right) standing before Philip II's granite bastion of the True Faith. As the dragon of heresy expires in the foreground, Saint Jerome, the Virgin, and Saint Lawrence cast their benedictions from above.*

palace. As James A. Michener observes in *Iberia,* his encyclopedic study of the peninsula and its peoples:

> Others who know Spanish architecture better than I condemn the building as an alien monstrosity. Where, they ask, . . . is the echo of Romanesque or Gothic, two styles that made themselves at home in Spain? And where in this enormous rectangle is there even a hint of the fact that Spain was for seven hundred years Moorish? . . .
>
> The traveler must make up his own mind in reference to his own experiences, and since most foreigners visiting Spain see the Gothic, the Romanesque and the Moorish and come to think of them as representing Spanish values, El Escorial must be a disappointment. Those like myself who have identified with Extremadura, and Las Marismas and the lonely plains of Castilla, have developed different visions of the country, and to these El Escorial conforms.

Modern tourists are likely to share at least some of Gautier's sentiments. Yet perhaps they will also agree with the English author of *A Guide to Spain and Portugal,* published in 1892:

> The Escorial must be considered . . . as the inspiration of a great mind tainted with melancholy, of deep piety, which sought rather to ponder on the sombre, awful, retributive side of religion, than on the sunnier one of mercy, hope, bliss, and love. The man explains the edifice, and the edifice is the picture of the man.

Those who can imagine, if not share, the deep fears and desperate hopes that Philip II's religious convictions brought to him and to the world of the sixteenth century will find they can penetrate the meaning of Philip's austere and enduring monument, El Escorial.

EL ESCORIAL
IN LITERATURE

DISENCHANTED TOURISTS

Over the centuries, El Escorial has attracted thousands of foreign visitors and inspired thousands of words of descriptive commentary. Among the better known of those travelers — and unquestionably among the better prose stylists of the genre — are the three chroniclers presented here: French drama critic Théophile Gautier, fellow Parisian Alexandre Dumas, and American diplomat and poet John Hay. In Gautier's A Romantic in Spain, *first published in 1843 as* Voyage en Espagne, *the renowned writer devotes several pages to his impressions of the Escorial, but the paragraphs below suffice to convey his opinion of Philip II's "desert of granite."*

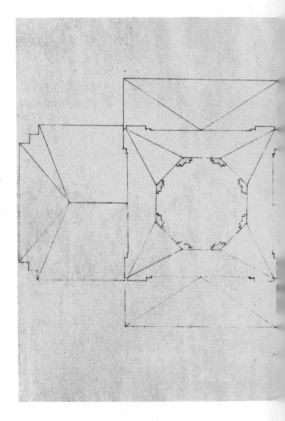

When I come to give an opinion of the Escorial, I am excessively perplexed. So many serious and highly placed persons — who, I prefer to think, had never seen it — have spoken of it as a masterpiece and a supreme achievement of human genius, that a poor devil of a wandering journalist like me will seem to be deliberately straining after originality, and taking a pleasure in running counter to accepted ideas; none the less, in my very soul and conscience, I cannot help considering the Escorial to be the dullest and most dismal building imagined for the mortification of their fellow-men by a gloomy monk and suspicion-haunted tyrant. I am well aware that the Escorial was destined for an austere religious purpose, but gravity is not the same thing as aridity, melancholy is not depression, contemplation is not tedium, and it is always possible happily to unite beauty of form with lofty ideals. . . .

The first thing which strikes you very unpleasantly is the ochreous yellow tone of the walls, which one might suppose to be built of compressed clay, if the joints of the stones, marked by lines of glaring white, did not prove the contrary. There could be no more monotonous sight than these six or seven-storied buildings, with no mouldings, no pilasters, and no columns, but with little crushed-looking windows, looking like the cells of a hive. It is the ideal of a barracks or a hospital; the only merit of it all is that it is built of granite. But this merit is thrown away, for at a hundred yards' distance it might be taken for potter's clay. . . . The façade does not stand out in any way from the bulk of the edifice, and in no way breaks its aridity. . . .

I came away from this desert of granite, this monkish necropolis, with an extraordinary sensation of satisfaction and relief; I felt as if I were being reborn, and might once again be young and rejoice in God's creation, all hope of which I had lost beneath these funereal vaults. The warm, luminous air enfolded me like a fine, downy woollen stuff, and infused a new warmth into my body, chilled by that atmosphere of death; I was delivered from that architectural nightmare which I had thought would never end. I advise those persons who have the idiocy to maintain that they are bored to go and pass three or four days at the Escorial; there they will discover what real tedium means, and will find amusement for the rest of their lives in the thought that they might be in the Escorial, but are not.

When we returned to Madrid there was a stir of pleased surprise among our friends, who were glad to see us still alive. Few people come back from the Escorial; they die of consumption in two or three days, or if by chance they are English, they blow their brains out. Luckily we have strong constitutions, and, as Napoleon said of the cannon ball which tried to knock him over, the building which is to be the death of us is not yet built.

THÉOPHILE GAUTIER
A Romantic in Spain, 1843

Alexandre Dumas, Gautier's contemporary, shared the latter's jaundiced view of the Escorial. In the following excerpt from his Adventures in Spain, *published in 1846, the author of such swashbuckling romances as* The Count of Monte Cristo *and* The Three Musketeers *records his visit to Philip II's monument. The "Madame" Dumas addresses has not been identified, but as his translator Alma Murch points out, "There were several ladies of Paris who must have missed him during his absence. . . ."*

The day dawned gray, overcast with cloud, and I was glad, for that seemed to me the right light in which to see the Escorial. At a turn of the road we caught sight of its sepulchral immensity, truly worthy of the man who chose the desert for his capital and a tomb for his palace. . . .

No one can imagine how austere, how mournful, the Escorial looks, a granite monument on a granite mountain, like some natural phenomenon. Approaching it, one realizes the insignificance of man in the face of its gigantic bulk. A great door yawns, then shuts behind you, and though you are merely a casual visitor, if you are aware of what freedom means to you, you shudder as though you were fated never to leave this place.

Nothing can give you any idea of the Escorial, not Windsor in England, nor Peterhoff in Russia, nor Versailles in France. It is like nothing but itself, created by a man who bent his epoch to his will, a reverie fashioned in stone, conceived during the sleepless hours of a king on whose realms the sun never set. No one could call it beautiful. It evokes not admiration, but terror. Even Philip himself must have shuddered when his architect handed him the thousand keys of this monument conjured up by his inflexible spirit.

Have you ever descended a mine and felt that a whole mountain was pressing down on you? That is how one feels on entering the Escorial. In other monuments, one climbs; in this, one descends. . . .

It is a strange thing, Madame, that whenever a powerful personality expresses itself in creating a masterpiece, strong as granite, that work is not left inviolate as a sacred memorial. Once in the course of centuries there comes a man, typical of his own times, the mirror of a whole epoch, who leaves behind him a monument to make his spirit known to all future generations. Then comes another man, weak and paltry, who cannot endure the sublime melancholy from which his predecessor drew strength, so he brings in some bungling dauber or tinsmith, saying to the first: "All this is too sad, too funereal for me, poor frivolous creature that I am. Paint me something pretty on these walls," and to the other: "Make me a nice bit of decoration to smarten up this staircase." So the dauber and the tinker set happily to work, and profane for all time the masterpiece they think to embellish. God have mercy on M. Andrieux who renovated *Nicomède*; and on King Charles II, who touched up the Escorial.

So, Madame, if ever you visit the Escorial, limit your sightseeing to three things, the chapel, the *Podridero* [burial vault], and the room where Philip died. All the rest would only weaken your first impressions. So rarely in life do we experience a profound sensation which, even while we tremble, opens new and strange horizons before our eyes, that I would never shrink from a deeply moving experience, even though it should drown me in sadness and terror as the Escorial has done.

ALEXANDRE DUMAS
Adventures in Spain, 1846

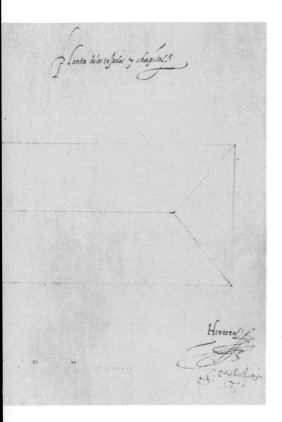

The sketches, elevations, and diagrams illustrating El Escorial in Literature *(pages 138–60) are the work of Juan de Herrera, the architect who oversaw the Escorial's construction for seventeen years. The signed diagram above reveals that the Escorial's basilica was originally designed in the shape of a Latin cross.*

During the last decades of the nineteenth century John Milton Hay pursued two simultaneous careers with equal success. Between 1860 and 1905 Hay served successively as private secretary to Abraham Lincoln, assistant secretary of state, ambassador to Great Britain, and finally as secretary of state under William McKinley and Theodore Roosevelt. These same years witnessed the emergence of Hay as a major American literary figure. A ten-volume biography of Lincoln, coauthored by Hay and released in 1890, capped a literary life that began in 1871, the year Hay published Castilian Days, *a droll account of his travels in Spain.*

There are few scenes in the world so depressing as that which greets you as you enter into the wide court before the church, called El Templo. You are shut finally in by these iron-gray walls. The outside day has given you up. Your feet slip on the damp flags. An unhealthy fungus tinges the humid corners with a pallid green. You look in vain for any trace of human sympathy in those blank walls and that severe façade. There is a dismal attempt in that direction in the gilded garments and the painted faces of the colossal prophets and kings that are perched above the lofty doors. But they do not comfort you; they are tinselled stones, not statues.

Entering the vestibule of the church, and looking up, you observe with a sort of horror that the ceiling is of massive granite and flat. The sacristan has a story that when Philip saw this ceiling, which forms the floor of the high choir, he remonstrated against it as too audacious, and insisted on a strong pillar being built to support it. The architect complied, but when Philip came to see the improvement he burst into lamentation, as the enormous column destroyed the effect of the great altar. The canny architect, who had built the pillar of pasteboard, removed it with a touch, and his majesty was comforted. Walking forward to the edge of this shadowy vestibule, you recognize the skill and taste which presided at this unique and intelligent arrangement of the choir. If left, as usual, in the body of the church, it would have seriously impaired that solemn and simple grandeur which distinguishes this above all other temples. There is nothing to break the effect of the three great naves, divided by immense square-clustered columns, and surmounted by the vast dome that rises with all the easy majesty of a mountain more than three hundred feet from the decent black and white pavement. I know of nothing so simple and so imposing as this royal chapel, built purely for the glory of God and with no thought of mercy or consolation for human infirmity. The frescos of Luca Giordano show the attempt of a later and degenerate age to enliven with form and color the sombre dignity of this faultless pile. But there is something in the blue and vapory pictures which shows that even the unabashed Luca was not free from the impressive influence of the Escorial.

A flight of veined marble steps leads to the beautiful retable of the high altar. The screen, over ninety feet high, cost the Milanese Trezzo seven years of labor. The pictures illustrative of the life of our Lord are by Tibaldi and Zuccaro. The gilt bronze tabernacle of Trezzo and Herrera, which has been likened with the doors of the Baptistery of Florence as worthy to figure in the architecture of heaven, no longer exists. It furnished a half hour's amusement to the soldiers of France. On either side of the high altar are the oratories of the royal family, and above them are the kneeling effigies of Charles, with his wife, daughter, and sisters, and Philip with his successive harem of wives. One of the few luxuries this fierce bigot allowed himself was that of

One of the towers of the basilica

a new widowhood every few years. There are forty other altars with pictures good and bad. The best are by the wonderful deaf-mute, Navarrete, of Logroño, and by Sanchez Coello, the favorite of Philip.

To the right of the high altar in the transept you will find, if your tastes . . . run in a bony direction, the most remarkable Reliquary in the world. With the exception perhaps of Cuvier, Philip could see more in a bone than any man who ever lived. In his long life of osseous enthusiasm he collected seven thousand four hundred and twenty-one genuine relics, — whole skeletons, odd shins, teeth, toenails, and skulls of martyrs, — sometimes by a miracle of special grace getting duplicate skeletons of the same saint. The prime jewels of this royal collection are the grilled bones of San Lorenzo himself, bearing dim traces of his sacred gridiron.

The sacristan will show you also the retable of the miraculous wafer, which bled when trampled on by Protestant heels at Gorcum in 1525. This has always been one of the chief treasures of the Spanish crown. The devil-haunted idiot Charles II made a sort of idol of it, building it this superb altar, consecrated "in this miracle of earth to the miracle of heaven." When the atheist Frenchmen sacked the Escorial and stripped it of silver and gold, the pious monks thought most of hiding this wonderful wafer, and when the storm passed by, the booby Ferdinand VII restored it with much burning of candles, swinging of censers, and chiming of bells. Worthless as it is, it has done one good work in the world. It inspired the altar-picture of Claudio Coello, the last best work of the last of the great school of Spanish painters. He finished it just before he died of shame and grief at seeing Giordano, the nimble Neapolitan, emptying his buckets of paint on the ceiling of the grand staircase, where St. Lawrence and an army of martyrs go sailing with a fair wind into glory.

JOHN MILTON HAY
Castilian Days, 1871

ROYALTY ENTOMBED

One of the earliest descriptions of the Escorial's Pantheon of the Kings, the octagonal jasper and marble crypt that houses the mortal remains of twenty-six Spanish monarchs, was written by Fray Francisco de los Santos, chaplain to Philip IV. The outspoken cleric's devotion to his master's predecessor, Philip III, is evident in the following excerpt. While lavishing praise upon the monarch who began the sumptuous Pantheon, the friar gently admonishes his son for having completed the task in a lamentably lackluster fashion.

The glory and crown of . . . [the Escorial] is the pantheon chapel, the sepulchre of the monarchs of Spain, and may indeed be termed the ne plus ultra of human power and art; for, neither the ancients, nor moderns, have produced a monument equal to it, though some have been placed among the wonders of the world; particularly the mausoleum of Artemisia in Caria, and the pyramids of Egypt, but both erected on the sandy basis of a wild and barbarous ostentation; whereas the foundation of this majestic repository of the kings of Spain, was catholic piety: accordingly the duration is permanent, and the lustre of their glory will shine to the latest posterity. The honor of the Almighty, and the respect to their progenitors, were the sole views of the illustrious founders. . . .

The principal, which induced Philip II to build the monastery of St.

Laurence, was the last command of his royal father, Charles V who, in a codicil signed at the convent of St. Jerom de Juste, left to him every particular relating to his burial, and that of the empress Isabella his consort, only desiring, that a receptacle might be made for himself, his empress, and all his successors. Philip accordingly formed the scheme of the Escurial, the glory of Spain, and wonder of the world; and certainly, a more signal proof of filial obedience was never seen. With the duty of a son, he blended the magnificence of a king; and as he had gained the appellation of the second Solomon, by a thousand acts of wisdom and munificence, and more especially, by the splendid church, or temple, he had erected; it was in his royal intention likewise to imitate the Jewish monarch in building an august sepulchre to his father, but was prevented by public difficulties. . . .

At the very bottom of the foundation, under the great altar, was constructed a spacious church of a circular form, with a proportionate cupola, altar, and a tribune facing it, for performing the offices; and in the sides, cavities for receiving the coffins. The descent to it, from the great chapel, was by two back stairs, and as many elegant marble stair-cases, one leading from the convent and sacristy, and the other from the palace; but it afterwards occurring to the founder's mind, that this was too distant, dark, and difficult of access, he gave orders for building a vault between this chapel, and the principal church, directly under the high altar. . . .

The fame of this astonishing structure, the vastness of its dimensions, the grandeur of its architecture, and the splendor of its decorations, drew an infinite number of persons of taste and distinction from all parts of Europe, who, amidst their raptures of applause, could not conceal their astonishment, at the meanness of the sepulchre, which contained such glorious monarchs, that they who had so enlarged the bounds of the christian world, should be confined in so narrow, so mean a repository. This was a very affecting remark, and raised pity in the breasts of many. . . . These remarks of foreigners, together with the injunctions of his father and grand-father, determined Philip III to undertake the pantheon; and he accordingly declared in public, that, immediately after he had finished some other works recommended to him in his father's last codicil, it should be commenced and conducted with all the dispatch consistent with its intended magnificence. . . .

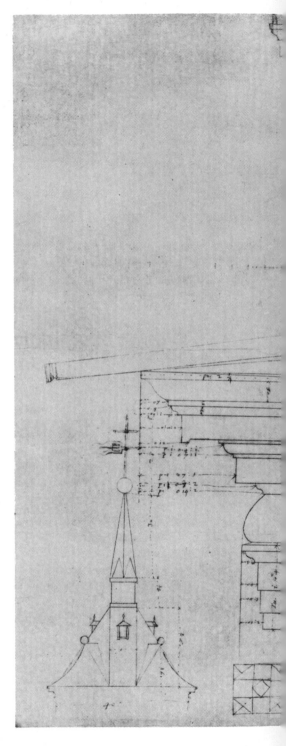

Vast quantities of jasper were brought from the quarries of Toledo, and those of Tortosa were drained of their marble. Such was the multitude of laborers, workmen, overseers, and other officers, that the work went on with incredible expedition, and within a few years, that pious prince, had not an untimely death prevented him, would have seen the accomplishment of his noble design, as within little more than three years, it was entirely paved, encrustated, and embellished with the most exquisite work in marble, jasper, and gilt brass, though still short of its ultimate perfection.

The cupola remaining to be covered; the arms and stair-cases were not finished; many of the bronzes were not cast, and few gilded; and, what was still worse, the former inconveniences, a want of light, and difficulty of access, still continued. It was indeed a misfortune, that, by the death of the king, its conclusion little agreed with its magnificent beginning; the usual fate of superb edifices, which generally remain as they were at the death of him who gave them existence.

FRAY FRANCISCO DE LOS SANTOS
A Description of the Escurial, c. 1650

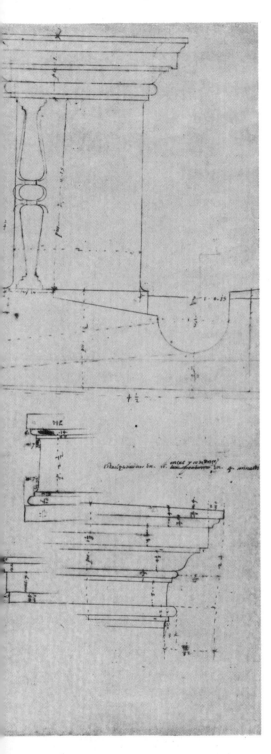

A working sketch of the cornice moldings for the Court of the Evangelists

The redoubtable Frances Erskine Inglis Calderón de la Barca, Scottish-born wife of a high-ranking Spanish diplomat, published The Attaché in Madrid *in 1856, during the turbulent aftermath of the Carlist War. In her frank and frequently reproving chronicle, Sra. Calderón de la Barca recorded the key events of those politically uncertain years with both wit and style. Her description of the inauspicious birth and untimely death of Isabella II's fourth daughter concludes with a reverent recounting of the ill-fated infanta's interment in the Escorial.*

The morning being bitterly cold, we drew up the windows, wrapped ourselves in our cloaks, ventured to light our cigars, and proceeded, of course at a very slow pace, behind the magnificent car containing the remains of the little Infanta.

In the villages of Las Rozas, Galapagar, and what is called the *Escorial de Abajo,* long delays were made. The clergy of the parish churches came out to meet the procession, and again the beautiful psalm, *Laudate pueri Dominum,* was entoned in solemn accents, under the clear blue cold sky. It was dusk long before we arrived at the Escorial, at nearly half-past six. I strained my eyes in the darkness to distinguish this wonderful monument of the stern Catholic monarch, into whose domains we thus entered in the darkness of the night, to deliver up, as it were, to his guardianship an innocent little descendant of his race. It loomed out in the darkness, immense, mysterious, lonely. The snowy crowns of the Guadarramas were distinctly visible. The wind blew fiercely, and sounded like a sad and moaning requiem, proceeding from the everlasting hills. The stars shone out clearly and coldly, through the dark clouds that were blown across their silvery disks.

. . . The procession moved slowly towards the monastery, and drew up in front of the royal chapel. The two masters of the horse descended the coffin from the hearse, and delivered it to the lords of the royal household, who placed it upon a kind of *estrade* [dais], prepared for its reception under the portico leading to the great entrance of the Spanish monarchs.

Here the scene was most striking; a long procession of chaplains and churchmen, headed by the abbot in his cope, the crucifix borne in front, advanced to meet the body.

Then the chaplain . . . read in a loud and distinct voice an order from their majesties, transmitted to the abbot by the patriarch of the Indies, in which they communicated to him the death of her serene highness the Infanta, desiring that her royal body, now transported to the Escorial, should be deposited with the usual solemnities. . . .

The procession entered the church, and it required little imagination to believe the whole scene a vision of by-gone ages. "A hut for myself, a palace for God," said the monarch who designed this glorious pile. I cannot pretend to describe it, for all was indistinct in gloom and grandeur. The blazing lights which yet but faintly illuminated the immense cathedral — the echo of the music, *Beati immaculati in via* — the abbot and priests — grandees and officers in uniform — all this preparation for receiving the remains of an infant who had scarcely opened her eyes on the light, but who was the descendant of a long line of princes — the immense magnitude of every thing in this gigantic temple, making the tallest men dwindle into pigmies by comparison — the whole produced an effect which no time can efface from my memory.

The procession proceeded, bearing the coffin, with all its rich adornings, and placed it upon a monument prepared for its reception in the centre of the church, upon the golden cushion, at the head of which was a royal crown; at each side numerous vases of flowers, and to the right and left eight tapers of white wax. On the high altar burned a huge bronze candelabra, destined exclusively for royal interments, with nine lighted torches. Though the whole edifice was illuminated, it still looked gloomy. When the prayers were concluded, the royal corps of monteros and the queen's guards received the body into their custody, and remained to keep watch over it during the night. I could not with propriety remain, as I would willingly have done, to examine the wonders of the church, so I took one glance at the little upturned waxen face of the Infanta, lying in her calm sleep, all unconscious of the royal honors paid her, left the guards to their cold and solemn night-watch, and followed the procession into the palace.

I must confess that the sight of a spacious tapestried hall, well lighted, at the further end of which was a roaring fire, of huge logs of wood, and of a long table covered with smoking dishes, brought me down to real life, and made me forget for a while every consideration but that of the intense cold and hunger from which I was suffering. . . .

As we drove off, I took one last look of the Escorial, now brilliantly illuminated by the morning sun! Alone in a desert, it can be compared with no surrounding object, unless with the lofty mountains behind it. The embodiment of a grand idea, a great and gloomy mind could alone have accomplished it. I promise myself to return hither in spring, yet it seems to me that winter is the most appropriate time for seeing the Escorial in all its stern gloom and grandeur.

FRANCES ERSKINE INGLIS CALDERÓN DE LA BARCA
The Attaché in Madrid, 1856

In 1849 American historian William Hickling Prescott began his History of the Reign of Philip the Second. *The brilliant Bostonian did not live to complete his projected four-volume work, but he did finish the third volume by 1858, the year before his death. Today that unfinished history is ranked with Prescott's classic works on Ferdinand and Isabella and on the conquests of Mexico and Peru — all products of the nearly blind scholar's lifelong devotion to the study of Spanish history.* Philip the Second, *written with a distinctive combination of liveliness and impeccable scholarship, ends with the construction of the king's "gloomy pile" of a palace. These selections from the final chapter give a poignant glimpse of Philip and his fourth wife, Anna, during their first — and her last — days at the Escorial.*

THROUGH THE EYES OF HISTORY

During the latter half of Philip's reign he was in the habit of repairing with his court to the Escorial and passing here a part of the summer. Hither he brought his young queen, Anne of Austria, — when the gloomy pile assumed an unwonted appearance of animation. [He had married Anna] . . . less than two years after he had consigned the lovely Isabella to the tomb. Anne had been already plighted to the unfortunate Don Carlos. Philip's marriage with her afforded him the melancholy triumph of a second time supplanting his son. She was his niece; for the Empress Mary, her mother, was the daughter of Charles the Fifth. There was, moreover, a great disparity in their years; for the Austrian princess, having been borne in Castile during the regency of her parents, in 1549, was at this time but twenty-

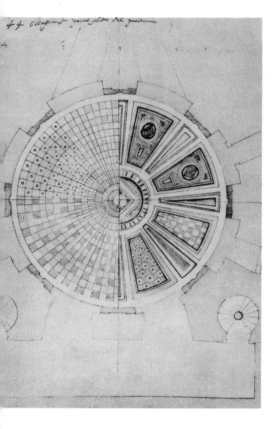

Rejected designs for the inlaid marble floor of the Pantheon of the Kings

one years of age, — less than half the age of Philip. It does not appear that her father, the Emperor Maximilian, made any objection to the match. If he felt any, he was too politic to prevent a marriage which would place his daughter on the throne of the most potent monarchy in Europe. . . .

As soon as the building of the Escorial was sufficiently advanced to furnish suitable accommodations for his young queen, Philip passed a part of every summer in its cloistered solitudes, which had more attraction for him than any other of his residences. The presence of Anne and her courtly train diffused something like an air of gayety over the grand but gloomy pile, to which it had been little accustomed. Among other diversions for her entertainment we find mention made of *autos sacramentales,* those religious dramas that remind one of the ancient Mysteries and Moralities which entertained our English ancestors. These *autos* were so much in favor with the Spaniards as to keep possession of the stage longer than in most other countries; nor did they receive their full development until they had awakened the genius of Calderon.

It was a pen, however, bearing little resemblance to that of Calderon which furnished these edifying dramas. They proceeded, probably, from some Jeronymite gifted with more poetic vein than his brethren. The actors were taken from among the pupils in the seminary established in the Escorial. Anne, who appears to have been simple in her tastes, is said to have found much pleasure in these exhibitions, and in such recreation as could be afforded her by excursions into the wild, romantic country that surrounded the monastery. Historians have left us but few particulars of her life and character, — much fewer than of her lovely predecessor. Such accounts as we have represent her as of an amiable disposition and addicted to pious works. She was rarely idle, and employed much of her time in needle-work, leaving many specimens of her skill in this way in the decorations of the convents and churches. . . .

Her wedded life was destined not to be a long one, — only two years longer than that of Isabella. She was blessed, however, with a more numerous progeny than either of her predecessors. She had four sons and a daughter. But all died in infancy or early childhood except the third son, who as Philip the Third lived to take his place in the royal dynasty of Castile.

The queen died on the twenty-sixth of October, 1580, in the thirty-first year of her age and the eleventh of her reign. A singular anecdote is told in connection with her death. This occurred at Badajoz, where the court was then established, as a convenient place for overlooking the war in which the country was at that time engaged with Portugal. While there the king fell ill. The symptoms were of the most alarming character. The queen, in her distress, implored the Almighty to spare a life so important to the welfare of the kingdom and of the Church, and instead of it to accept the sacrifice of her own. Heaven, says the chronicler, as the result showed, listened to her prayer. The king recovered; and the queen fell ill of a disorder which in a few days terminated fatally. Her remains, after lying in state for some time, were transported with solemn pomp to the Escorial, where they enjoyed the melancholy pre-eminence of being laid in the quarter of the mausoleum reserved exclusively for kings and the mothers of kings. Such was the end of Anne of Austria, the fourth and last wife of Philip the Second.

WILLIAM HICKLING PRESCOTT
History of the Reign of Philip the Second, 1855-58

In 1960, another distinguished American scholar, Garrett Mattingly, won a Pulitzer special citation for The Armada, *his history of Philip II's ill-fated campaign against England. In chapter 33, set in "The Escurial, New Year's, 1589," Mattingly describes Philip's reaction to news of the armada's defeat.*

Imperturbability in the face of triumph or disaster was a part of the public character of Philip II, a part of his legend in his lifetime. As a small boy he must have heard many times how his father, the emperor, had received the news of the great victory at Pavia with a self-restraint which had aroused universal admiration. Probably he resolved to emulate such behavior, and found it the easier to do so because his temperament was naturally something less than effervescent. At any rate, by the thirty-third year of his reign, Philip had become, for his many admirers, the typical Christian stoic, and a hundred popular stories illustrated his admirable self-control under trying circumstances. Some were like the comic classic about the newly appointed secretary who was so nervous in his unfamiliar duties that when he took a freshly written sheet from the king's hand, instead of sanding it, he poured the inkhorn over it. He cringed in expectation of the royal wrath, only to be told gently, "*That* is the *ink. This* is the sand." Some were like the pathetic anecdotes of the king's long-suffering patience with the growing eccentricity of his first-born son and heir, Don Carlos. There were so many such stories current within a decade of Philip's death that naturally some of his more sympathetic chroniclers found some to illustrate his iron self-control at the moment of his greatest disappointment.

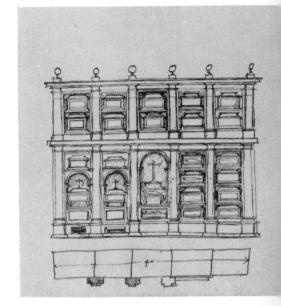

Father Famiano Strada's apologue has the highest literary polish. As he tells it, the king was still nourishing the belief that the Armada was victorious when a courier from Santander (Maestre de campo Bobadilla?) reached the Escurial with the news of disaster. The royal secretaries, Moura and Idiáquez, were aghast, and each tried to persuade the other to break the evil tidings. Finally Moura entered the royal cabinet and when the king laid down his pen and looked up, the secretary stammered something about bad news of the Armada, and thrust the courier forward. The king listened to the dismal tale without a change of countenance and when it was ended, said, "I give thanks to God by whose hand I have been so endowed that I can put to sea another fleet as great as this we have lost whenever I choose. It does not matter if a stream is sometimes choked, as long as the source flows freely." And without a sigh or a change of expression, the king picked up his pen and went on with his letters.

But Strada was, after all, Roman born and bred, and Spanish eloquence at its best is less ornate and has a deeper, more iron-throated clang. Perhaps that is why, from the later seventeenth century on, Spanish historians preferred a variant version. The build-up, the frightened secretaries, the serenely toiling king, the courier's grim news, all these are the same, but before he takes up his pen again, the king says only: "I sent my ships to fight against men and not against the winds and waves of God."

Rough sketches of the Altar of Reliquaries at the Escorial

None of these stories, of course, could possibly be true. Philip had no opportunity to display his famous constancy in the face of unexpected disaster because the full extent of the defeat was broken to him by slow degrees. Some time before the duke made Santander, Philip had read Medina Sidonia's letter of August 21st with its accompanying *Diario,* and listened to Captain Baltazar de Zúñiga's depressing report. He had heard both

Parma's account of the missed rendezvous and, later, rumors of wrecks on the Irish coast. Nor is it believable that Philip would so instantaneously have blamed the winds and waves of the God his fleet had sailed to serve, especially since he had learned from Medina Sidonia's *Diario* that, up to August 21st, anyway, the Armada had had all the best of it in the way of weather.

That Philip faced the bad news, as it came in, with dignity and constancy one can well believe, though there are limits to the constancy that can be expected of any human frame. He was seriously ill that fall, an illness, in the opinion of the diplomatic corps, brought on, or at least aggravated, by anxiety and disappointment. The new papal nuncio thought that the king's eyes were red from weeping as well as from study, though if Philip wept, no one saw him. And there were those to say that the events of the past ten months had aged the king as many years. It is after 1588 that his skin begins to have that curious mushroom pallor and to hang on his face in pouches. The beard loses the last hint of yellow in its white — is longer, and in some portraits looks curiously neglected. After 1588 the king went outdoors less often, saw fewer and fewer people, worked longer and longer in his solitary study.

But if Philip felt the blow of fate, and showed he felt it, he was not crushed by it. Almost as soon as he learned the extent of his losses he was assuring ambassadors that he would build another fleet stronger than the last, if he had to melt down every piece of plate on his table and every silver candlestick in the Escurial.

GARRETT MATTINGLY
The Armada, 1959

VISITORS FROM AFAR

Confessing that "a passion for Spanish things" had dominated his boyhood, American man-of-letters William Dean Howells set about describing his 1911 visit to the Iberian Peninsula in a volume entitled Familiar Spanish Travels. *Howells's account of his sojourn in Spain is suffused with the same combination of literacy and gusto that marked the prolific writer's long career as author, editor, playwright, and poet.*

It seems a duty every Protestant owes his heresy to go and see how dismally the arch-enemy of heresy housed his true faith in the palace-tomb-and-church of the Escorial. If the more light-minded tourist shirks this act of piety, he makes a mistake which he will repent afterward in vain. The Escorial is, for its plainness, one of the two or three things worthiest seeing . . . in Spain. . . .

It is the distinct merit of the Escorial that it does not, and perhaps cannot take long in doing; otherwise the doer could not bear it. A look round the sumptuous burial chamber of the sovereigns below the high altar of the church; a glance at the lesser sepulchral glories of the infantes and infantas in their chapels and corridors, suffices for the funereal third of the trinity of tomb and temple and palace; and though there are gayer constituents of the last, especially the gallery of the chapter-house, with its surprisingly lively frescoes and its sometimes startling canvases, there is not much that need really keep you from the royal apartments which seem the natural end of your visit. Of these something better can be said than that they are no worse than most other royal apartments; our guide led us to them through many granite courts and corridors where we left groups of unguided Americans still maddening over their Baedekers; and we found them hung with pleasing tapestries, some after such designs of Goya's as one finds in the basement of the Prado. The furniture was in certain rooms cheerily upholstered in crimson and salmon without sense of color, but as if seeking relief from the gray of the church; and there are battle-pieces on the walls, fights between Moors and Christians, which interested me. The dignified consideration of the custodian who showed us through the apartments seemed to have adapted to our station a manner left over from the infrequent presence of royalty; as I have said, the young king of Spain does not like coming to the Escorial. . . .

. . . I am not going to leave the Escorial to the reader without trying to make him feel that I too was terribly impressed by it. To be sure, I had some light moments in it, because when gloom goes too far it becomes ridiculous; and I did think the convent gardens as I saw them from the chapter-house window were beautiful, and the hills around majestic and serious, with no intention of falling upon my prostrate spirit. Yes, and after a lifelong abhorrence of that bleak king who founded the Escorial, I will own that I am, through pity, beginning to feel an affection for Philip II; perhaps I was finally wrought upon by hearing him so endearingly called Philly by our guide.

Yet I will not say but I was glad to get out of the Escorial alive; and that I welcomed even the sulkiness of the landlord of the hotel where our guide took us for lunch. To this day I do not know why that landlord should have been so sour; his lunch was bad, but I paid his price without murmuring; and still at parting he could scarcely restrain his rage; the Escorial might have entered into his soul. On the way to his hotel the street was empty, but the house bubbled over with children who gaped giggling at his guests from the kitchen door, and were then apparently silenced with food, behind it. There were a great many flies in the hotel, and if I could remember its name I would warn the public against it.

WILLIAM DEAN HOWELLS
Familiar Spanish Travels, 1913

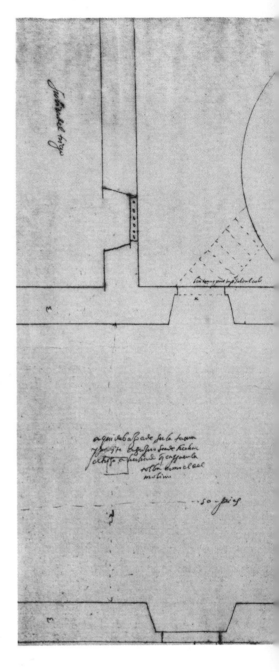

In the preface to A Sampler of Castile, *English artist and critic Roger Fry asserts that his slim work is nothing more than a collection of "variegated, vivid, and odd impressions" — in short, a book written "for myself." Fry's narrative is anything but self-indulgent, however, and his observations clearly merit wider circulation than they received in 1923 when Leonard and Virginia Woolf produced a handsomely bound, limited edition of Fry's* Sampler *for their Bloomsbury circle.*

Every one agrees that the Escorial is one of the most impressive sights of Spain. Surely no king has ever left a sharper imprint of his spirit than Philip II. Gloomy and bigoted that spirit may have been, but it was not, I imagine, without a kind of genius. For genius must lurk somewhere behind this strange conception of a royal residence and monastery rolled into one and called into monstrous being on the lonely slopes of the Guadarrama. Was it wrong, I wonder, to see it, as I did, under ragged skies and soaked with a perpetual downpour of chilly rain, or was not that the way to understand how Philip felt? Anyhow, those uncompromising cold stone cloisters and dingy violet hills seemed curiously northern. On the desolate side of a Yorkshire moor there stands just such another grey, stone, cloistered court

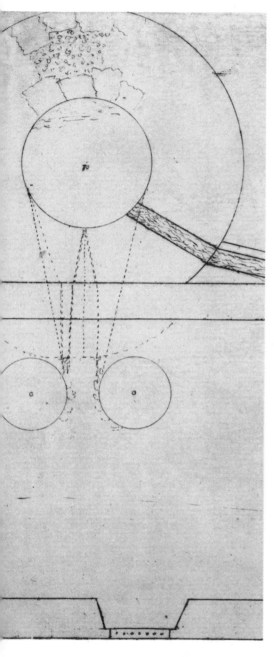

Design for the mill at the monastery

built by a Quaker of the eighteenth century for a charitable school. I kept on remembering it at Escorial, so similar a language did Catholic and Quaker puritanism find to express themselves in. Plainness is their common idiom, though the plainness of the one was practical and philanthropic and the plainness of the other grandiose and mystical. Certainly the Escorial is plain to the extreme, and not all Luca Giordano's flighty improvisations on its ceilings avail even to mitigate its austerity. Only perhaps in that suite of rooms where Goya's tapestries have found a home is the joy of life admitted. But would Philip have let Goya in? Would his instinctive good taste or his puritanism have won the day? It would have been a hard battle. No, what stays in one's memory are granite vaults of immaculate simplicity of curve and purity of surface, granite pilasters and narrow winding staircases, and everywhere the same grey, unyielding, gritty surface. One remembers most of all Herrera's great attempt, the church of S. Lorenzo. For once a Spanish artist is out to pit himself deliberately against a great Italian. For Herrera has definitely attempted to design in a Michelangelesque idiom. He has aimed at the great Italian architect's effects of sublimity in the proportions of his colossal pilasters, and at something of his sharpness of definition in the saliences of architrave and moulding, and at his concentration and close-knit unity of design. And no doubt up to a point he has succeeded; the effect is of tremendous mass and overpowering weight, the circular forms of arch and dome are well related to the sparse, emphatic, perpendiculars and the lateral proportions are clearly and definitely established. In fact he has been able to grasp so much of the Italian tradition of the High Renaissance and early Baroque as to enable him to be really impressive. As far as that general scenic effect on the casual spectator goes he can carry the style, and that, after all, is just what almost all Spanish religious art aimed at. It always had the effect on the worshippers' mind in view; how to overawe and impress him was the great concern. But for that very reason Herrera went no further. So that when once the first genuine shock of wonder which one feels on entering has worn off, the longer one looks the less impressive it becomes. There is here no such idea of perfection as haunted and urged on the Italians of the Cinque Cento. The sequences of relief are good enough for effect but not for contemplation. The proportions are good, but they are not finally and entirely inevitable. No further correspondences, no unexpected subtleties of sequence reveal themselves as one goes on looking. It is a skilful enough adaptation of ideas but not a great creation. If this is too severe it is because this building so definitely challenges the great Italians, and against them it cannot hold.

But perhaps it is better to accept what there is, and above all to admire the relentless conviction of the general idea of the building, the monotonous gravity and asceticism of its endless courts and cloisters and corridors. The influence of such constant repetition is overwhelming, and all seems designed to lead up to the culminating effect of the mausoleum below the High Altar. For to Philip's mind death must have been the central and dominating theme. And so down there the austerity at last relaxes; all that has been denied to life is reserved to give fitting honour to death. Gold and chiselled metal and rare polished marble make of this octagonal room with its elaborate dome a place of shining and dreadful luxury.

ROGER ELIOT FRY
A Sampler of Castile, 1923

The Greek poet and novelist Nikos Kazantzakis used the occasion of his visit to the Escorial for some wry and rather lugubrious speculations on the nature of Philip II's immortal soul. The following comments are from Spain, *published in Athens in 1957, the year of Kazantzakis's death.*

There is a little church in honor of [Saint Lawrence], wedged in among the precipitous rocks of the Escorial, 60 kilometers northwest of Madrid. Philip II had vowed that if he was victorious in battle, he would build a great monastery and dedicate it to Saint Lawrence. He was victorious, and in 1563 he began to carry out his vow. The pale fanatic king wanted to construct a house for his soul — a sheath to hold his cold strange brain. He cared nothing for the beauties and joys of this world. He refused to soothe his agony with curves and superfluous designs and bagatelles, such as please the carnal eye. He wished to carve in granite a fierce cave for his soul to burrow away. . . .

Would his soul be saved? Would it one day awake and bore through the gray stone walls, and fly like a yellow butterfly up over the enormous flower of God? Philip . . . watched the green and yellow blocks of granite joined and sealed, fitting out his final place of refuge. Ill and pallid-lipped, he went on watching in despair. What was the secret of this great king who never smiled?

Today as I was crossing the great courtyard of the Escorial, recollecting the fate of this tragic Othello of the Church, I suddenly remembered an old biography of one of the saints: Saint John the Faster was on his deathbed, in his hermit's cell in the desert. Off on the other side of the desert, Saint Nile learned the black tidings from an angel. He rose, took up his stick, but, owing to his great old age, he could not move. His disciples lifted him onto a stretcher, and so they carried him wrapped in his rags and all rolled up like a ball to his friend the hermit, who was in the pangs of death. "Quickly! Quickly!" Nile cried out along the way, thumping his stick. "Quickly! I must get to him while he's still alive!" But he did not get to him in time. The hermit had already died. Nile bent over to give him the last embrace. And then — lo! a miracle! says the biography — Saint John raised himself slightly and whispered something in Nile's ear, then straightway fell back again, dead.

In terror, Nile's disciples rushed over to kiss the hands and feet of their Master. They asked him: "What did he tell you? What did he tell you? Your eyes are dazed with horror, Holy Father!" But Nile did not want to confess anything. He never told the secret to any man. His life did not change in any way. Only from that time on, his lips never smiled again.

And today in the Escorial, suddenly a satanic thought tore through my mind and made it all as clear as day. I knew what the hermit had told him. I had found the secret! Saint John the Faster had murmured into the ear of his friend and companion in agony: "Brother, we are doomed! There is no Paradise!"

A Spaniard could bear this terrible revelation and go on living unperturbed, as if he had heard nothing; as if he could still hope; as if he were not certain of his doom. Philip, however, was a Hapsburg and he had not heard anything. Perhaps only in this icy piercing air of the Sierra Guadarrama could he sense these bitter forebodings. And that is why he was no longer able to laugh.

NIKOS KAZANTZAKIS
Spain, 1957

VICTORIAN BARDS

In 1860 a twenty-year-old Oxford undergraduate named John Addington Symonds won his college's coveted Newdigate Prize for poetry with a lengthy work called The Escorial. *That poem opens with a description of Philip's "palace of the dead" as it appeared after its sack by the French. The measured cadence of mid-Victorian rhyme seems especially suitable for a depiction of the plundered palace's monotonous façade, as excerpts from the English essayist's early effort suggest.*

Watching from Guadarrama's iron steep
The tardy morn along the valley creep,
Robed with dark pines I saw beneath me spread
Escorial's cloistered palace of the dead.
Deep in that dark which ushers in the day
The sombre piles of ashy granite lay, . . .

Lorn and forsaken on the quarried waste,
Her pride dishonoured, and her pomp effaced;
Yet does her front unscathed with scorn defy
Time's wasting hand: she bears her crown as high
As when those massive basements were first set,
Those vast arcades and cloisters arched with jet.
Perchance some ghastlier horror creeps and clings
Round gates which guard the sepulchre of kings;
With harsher moan the rusty hinges call,
And hollower echoes wake the vacant hall:
For now the shrines, the palace courts are still —
No sounds of banquet through their chambers thrill:
Round nave and choir no full-voiced organs sweep,
No black-stoled monks their holy vigils keep.
Yet, though the dust of ages drape her thrones,
Though ruin scowl above her cold grey stones,
Though shattered shrines and ravaged pomp betray
The Frenchman's rage, the vengeance of Houssaye:
Still wintry storms unheeded vex her crown,
From barren ridge and snow-field eddying down;
The plash of rain, the rending thunder shock
Alike in vain assail her stubborn rock:
Like some proud Queen of robe and circlet spoiled,
She grimly smiles and mocks her conqueror foiled.

Thus as I mused, from Eastern gates the sky
Flushed into purple, for the sun was nigh.
On clear cut angles floods of glory stole,
Round each swart tower flamed forth its aureole:
In sudden light the mass transfigured seemed
Radiant with beauty from the Past redeemed:
Then, as my gaze roved o'er the brightening plain,
Fancy sped forth o'er Memory's darker reign —
Pierced through the gloom that o'er Espagna lowers,
Revived her buried kings and built again her towers.

JOHN ADDINGTON SYMONDS
The Escorial, 1860

Among Herrera's more polished drawings is this detailed elevation of the Altar of Reliquaries in the nave.
    Overleaf:
A free-hand sketch of the basilica shows the four central piers and, above them, the steps leading to the High Altar.

151

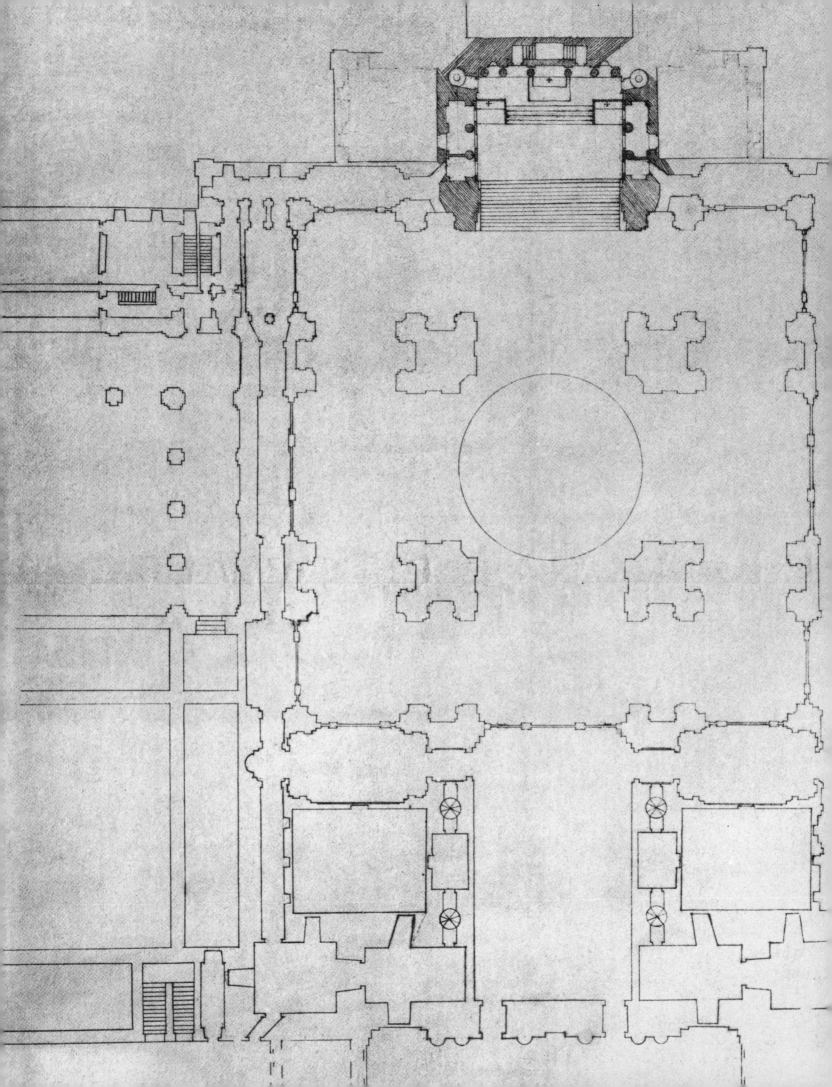

By coincidence, another young poet destined to achieve eminence during the latter half of the nineteenth century also published a poem entitled The Escorial *in 1860. Gerard Manley Hopkins was only fifteen years old when he composed his work, and its somewhat labored but abundantly detailed style clearly reflects the author's youth, enthusiasm, and inexperience. In successive stanzas, Hopkins diligently depicts the full history of the "eighth wonder of the earth" — beginning with its conception on the battlefield at Saint-Quentin.*

There is a massy pile above the waste
Amongst Castilian barrens mountain-bound;
A sombre length of grey; four towers placed
At corners flank the stretching compass round;
A pious work with threefold purpose crown'd —
A cloister'd convent first, the proudest home
Of those who strove God's gospel to confound
With barren rigour and a frigid gloom —
Hard by a royal palace and a royal tomb.

They tell its story thus; amidst the heat
Of battle once upon St. Lawrence' day
Philip took oath, while glory or defeat
Hung in the swaying of the fierce melée,
'So I am victor now, I swear to pay
The richest gift St. Lawrence ever bore,
When chiefs and monarchs came their gifts to lay
Upon his altar, and with rarest store
To deck and make most lordly evermore.'

For that staunch saint still prais'd his Master's name
While his crack'd flesh lay hissing on the grate;
Then fail'd the tongue; the poor collapsing frame,
Hung like a wreck that flames not billows beat —
So, grown fantastic in his piety,
Philip, supposing that the gift most meet,
The sculptured image of such faith would be,
Uprais'd an emblem of that fiery constancy.

He rais'd the convent as a monstrous grate;
The cloisters cross'd with equal courts betwixt
Formed bars of stone; beyond in stiffen'd state
The stretching palace lay as handle fix'd.
Then laver'd founts and postur'd stone he mix'd
   — Before the sepulchre there stood a gate,
A faithful guard of inner darkness fix'd —
But open'd twice, in life and death, to state,
To newborn prince, and royal corse inanimate. . . .

No finish'd proof was this of Gothic grace
With flowing tracery engemming rays
Of colour in high casements face to face;
And foliag'd crownals (pointing how the ways

Of art best follow nature) in a maze
Of finish'd diapers, that fills the eye
And scarcely traces where one beauty strays
And melts amidst another; ciel'd on high
With blazon'd groins, and crowned with hues of
   majesty.

This was no classic temple order'd round
With massy pillars of the Doric mood
Broad-fluted, nor with shafts acanthus-crown'd,
Pourtray'd along the frieze with Titan's brood
That battled Gods for heaven; brilliant-hued,
With golden fillets and rich blazonry,
Wherein beneath the cornice, horsemen rode
With form divine, a fiery chivalry —
Triumph of airy grace and perfect harmony. . . .

The rang'd long corridors and cornic'd halls,
And damasqu'd arms and foliag'd carving piled —
With painting gleamed the rich pilaster'd walls —
There play'd the virgin mother with her Child
In some broad palmy mead, and saintly smiled,
And held a cross of flowers in purple bloom;
He, where the crownals droop'd, himself reviled
And bleeding saw. — There hung from room to room
The skill of dreamy Claude, and Titian's mellow gloom.

GERARD MANLEY HOPKINS
The Escorial, 1860

ROYAL CONSPIRACIES

In his famous tragedy Don Carlos, *first presented in 1787, Germany's greatest playwright, Friedrich Schiller, portrayed the Escorial's founder as a tyrannical dictator, as cold and unyielding as his granite monument. The play, in which Schiller took certain liberties with historical fact, concerns the stormy relationship between Philip II and his son and heir Don Carlos — specifically the latter's political ambitions, his love for his father's young queen, and his ultimate execution by Philip. In Act II, Scene 2, Don Carlos has come to beg the king (who already suspects him of both moral and political treason) for more responsibility in the affairs of the crown.*

CARLOS   My father! now indeed again my father! My soul pours forth its thanks for his favour! — Give me your hand, my father — O delicious day! — The pleasure of his kiss has long been unknown to your son — But why? Oh! why? How do the wounds my soul has suffered bleed afresh at the thought: Why have I been so long banished from your heart? What have I done? O base suspicion! how dost thou perpetually corrode the hearts of kings, and sever the strong bonds of sacred instinct! Is it possible! Three-and-twenty years has the world called me Philip's son, yet does he not seem to know that he is my father.

PHILIP   Prince, thou are not well acquainted with these arts — practice them not; I want them not.

A precise rendering of an arched façade

CARLOS *(Rising)* Is this my answer? — In it I hear the voice of your courtly sycophants. Oh, my father! all is not true, by Heavens it is not! that a priest may say, or that the creatures of a priest may say. I am not vicious: the ardour of my blood is alone my fault, and youth my only offence. My heart may swell with violent emotions, but my heart is good.

PHILIP Thy heart is pure, I know it, as thy prayer.

CARLOS If I mean deceit, so may the Redeemer of the world cast me with wrath from his presence. My soul assumes an ardent confidence. Now if ever must be the time. We are alone. The shackles of state and ceremonial are fallen off, and a ray of hope, a delicious expectation, breaks in upon my heart — Methinks the angels of heaven, the beatified powers which surround the eternal throne, look with attention and pleasure on this important scene. Oh, my father! — Reconciliation! *(Falls at his feet.)*

PHILIP Rise, and leave me.

CARLOS Reconciliation!

PHILIP *(Attempting to loose himself from him.)* This buffoonery is too bold.

CARLOS Too bold! The love of thy child too bold?

PHILIP What! thy eyes filled with tears! Contemptible! Out of my sight.

CARLOS Now if ever — Reconciliation, my father!

PHILIP Begone — Return from my battles covered with dust and wounds, my arms shall be opened to receive thee — But when thus, I cast thee from me. *(Pushes him from him.)* Cowardly guilt alone washes itself disgracefully in such fountains. He who does not blush to repent, will not hesitate to commit what needs repentance.

CARLOS *(Surveys the King for some time with a mixture of fear and astonishment.)* By what mistake has this alien from human nature been mixed with mankind? Tears are the bond of humanity. His eye is dry; he was not born of woman. He knows not the sweet joy of weeping, which can express pleasure from torture, render misery enviable, exalt men to heaven, and bring down angels to mortality. Oh! constrain those yet unmoistened eyes timely to shed tears, before some heavy hour approaches when thou mayst want them.

PHILIP Dost thou think to dissipate the serious doubts of thy father by flimsy words?

CARLOS Doubts! I will exterminate these doubts — will forcibly appeal to my father's heart till I shall eradicate them. Who are those who have deprived me of the favour of my sovereign? What has the monk offered to the father for his son? What recompence will Alba make him for a childless deserted life — Wishest thou love? Here in this bosom is a spring of it, more fresh, more ardent, than can be found in the muddy stagnant reservoirs which must first be opened by Philip's gold.

PHILIP Desist from this rashness. The men you would scandalize are the tried servants of my choice, the supports of my throne; and wouldst thou, arrogant boy! wouldst thou impeach their honour?

CARLOS No more! I feel my powers. Whatever services Alba can render, Carlos can do the same, and more. What cares the hireling for that kingdom which never shall be his own? What cares he though the grey hairs of Philip turn white? His king remains when Philip is no more, and his coin will still be current — Your Carlos loves you — Oh! much should I dread to be alone and unbefriended when on a throne.

PHILIP *(As if struck by these words, remains for some time silent and thoughtful: after a pause.)* I am alone.

CARLOS *(Approaching him with animation and warmth.)* You have been so; but hate me no more; and I will love you as your child; will love you ardently; but hate me no more. Oh, how enchanting is it to know that we are honoured by a generous heart; that our joys communicate animation to other countenances; and our sufferings moisten with tears other eyes! How noble, how delightful! hand in hand with a beloved son to tread back again the rosy path of youth, and dream again the dream of life! How delicious to reflect, that in the virtues of our children our benevolence may be continued for ages! and we return to posterity in our sons as the luminary of day again arises on the world reflected by the mirror of night! How sweet to plant what a beloved son may reap; to gather what he shall employ for his benefit, and imagine the warm thankfulness of his grateful heart! Oh, this is an earthly paradise, of which your monks very wisely told you not.

PHILIP *(With emotion.)* O my son, my son, thou pronouncest thy own sentence. How enchantingly dost thou paint that happiness thou never wilt bestow upon me.

CARLOS To the Almighty I appeal — Yourself, yourself have excluded me both from approaching the government and all share in a father's heart, until now, until this day. Oh! was that kind; was that just? I the heir to the throne of Spain, am a stranger in Spain; a prisoner where I am to be a sovereign. Is that just; is that kind? — Oh! how often have I blushed to think that the envoys of foreign potentates, or the common gazettes of the time, should first bring to me at Aranjuez the news of what passed at the court! Then would I say, jestingly, with a heavy heart, "The King removes his son thus from public affairs, that when he mounts the throne his pleasure may be heightened by surprise."

PHILIP *(Surveying him earnestly.)* Carlos, you speak very frequently of that time when I shall be no more.

CARLOS No, by the Maker of us both; only of that when I shall be a man. Who is to blame if they are the same?

PHILIP It is an honourable office, my son, which thou hast assumed — the careful numberer of thy father's hours. Is this thy gratitude to him who gave thee life, perpetually to remind him of his death?

CARLOS *(Interrupting him with warmth.)* Give me employment, my father! and may your reign continue till the final doom of the world.

PHILIP Wait more experience. Your blood flows as yet too hastily through your veins. You would only do mischief.

CARLOS My blood indeed flows hastily! Three-and-twenty years have I been King Philip's son, and nothing has been entrusted to me either to build or to destroy. My heirship to the throne rouses me from my slumber like a rigid creditor; and all the lost hours of my youth call me aloud. The moment is come when this great debt of honour should be paid with interest. Future history, the renown of my ancestors, and the thundering trump of fame, all call me. The time is come when I should strive for the palm of glory — Gracious sovereign, may I prefer the petition which brought me hither.

Observing what both men already know — that the Duke of Alba has been ordered north to suppress the revolt of the Netherlands — Don Carlos begs to be put in command of that army. "It is the first request I have made in my life," he pleads. "Entrust Flanders to my government."

156

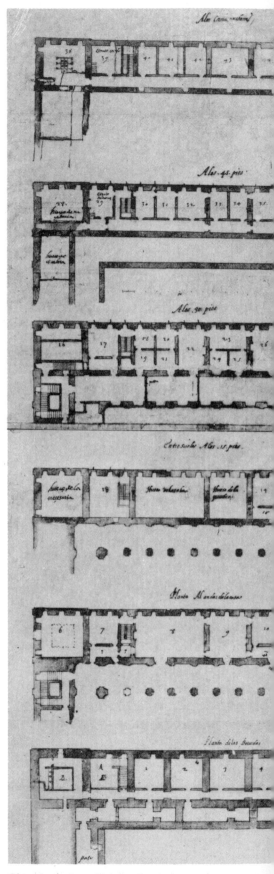

Six plans for the royal apartments

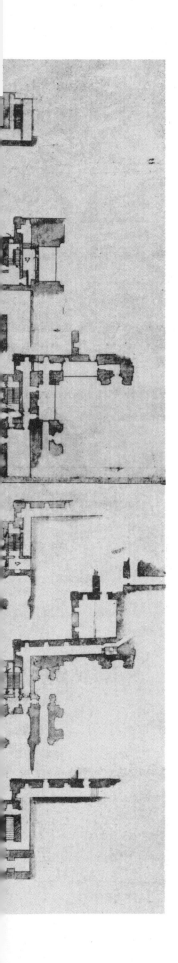

PHILIP *(After a long pause, during which he surveys his son with a piercing look.)* And at the same time my choicest army to your ambition; the dagger to my murderer!

CARLOS *(Retreating with great emotion.)* O gracious God! and is this all, this all the fruit of this long sought, this promising opportunity! *(After some pause, with milder earnestness.)* Answer me not so harshly. Send me not thus away. With this cruel answer dismiss me not, nor with this heavy heart. Answer me less harshly. Do some act which may awaken my filial duty, and bind me to you eternally your debtor. . . . [I] request that you . . . entrust to me the government of Flanders. Leave Spain I must, and will. A malady none suspect, rages within me. While here, I live as on the rack. The very air of Madrid is as insupportable to me as conscience to the murderer. An immediate change of climate alone can effect my cure. Send me immediately to Flanders.

PHILIP *(With continued calmness.)* Patients like thee, my son, require careful treatment, and to be continually under the eye of the physician. Thou shalt stay in Spain. The Duke goes to Flanders.

CARLOS *(In a kind of frenzy.)* Now guard me, good spirits.

PHILIP *(Retreating a step backward.)* What mean those extravagant gestures!

CARLOS *(In a faltering voice.)* My father, is your determination irrevocable?

PHILIP It is that of the King.

CARLOS Then I have done. *(Makes a reverence and is retiring.)*

PHILIP *(Looks stedfastly on him some time, without speaking, then calls him back.)* Prince, this silent departure is not submission.

CARLOS No.

PHILIP No?

CARLOS I at that moment imagined I saw the testament of the emperor, your father, smoking on a pile.

PHILIP *(Starting.)* Ha! What means that?

CARLOS So great a man! So perfect an emperor! and shall the insect complain! — I received, but he gave — and how infinitely much is wanting for me to be such a son as he was a father! *(Exit.)*

PHILIP *(Covers his face and strikes his breast.)* Too heavily, O God, lies thy hand upon me. — My son — Oh, my son!

FRIEDRICH SCHILLER
Don Carlos, 1787

Benito Pérez Galdós, Spain's leading nineteenth-century novelist, used the Escorial as the setting to tell of a later conspiracy — Prince Ferdinand's alleged plot with Napoleon to unseat his father, Charles IV. The work, entitled The Court of Charles IV: A Romance of the Escorial, *was published in 1873. Ostensibly the diary of a young servant, it is actually a fairly realistic treatment of the intrigues of the Spanish court on the eve of the Napoleonic invasion of 1808.*

As on our arrival at the Escorial we were startled by finding that some very important events had happened, the reader will not think it superfluous that I should report what I had heard during the journey from the Marquesa's house-steward, for subsequent facts gave his words a prophetic meaning.

"It strikes me," said he, "that something is going on at the Palace which will make a noise in the world. They said in Madrid this morning. — However, we shall soon know all there is to be known, for within three hours and a half, God willing, we shall cast anchor in the courtyard."

"But what were they saying at Madrid?"

"In the city every one is for the Prince and hates the King and Queen; and it seems that their Majesties have determined to quell the lad by keeping him always with them. I have seen that myself, and the Prince's face is enough to make you pity him. — They say his parents do not love him, which is a great shame; and I have been assured that the King has not once taken him out hunting, and does not admit him to sit at his table nor show him any of the kindness that seems natural in a good father."

"So that the Prince has become entangled in some conspiracy or plot?" said I.

"It may very well be. From what I heard last week at the Palace, the Prince has retired altogether from society; he talks to no one and goes about like a man who sees visions, passing whole nights out of bed. The Court are greatly alarmed at this, and it seems they have set people to watch him till they have discovered what he has got in hand."

"But I remember that I have heard say that the Prince is studious, and that he spends the night in translating from French or Latin, I forget which exactly."

"Yes; that is what is said at the Escorial; but, God knows! — Some say that the Prince is plotting big things: that in marching his troops into Spain Napoleon has nothing further from his thoughts than an attack on Portugal, but has sent them to support the Prince's party."

"That is all talk. Perhaps poor young Ferdinand thinks of nothing but his books. . . ."

"But it seems that his translation lately met with his Papa's and Mamma's disapproval, for it related to some revolution; so now he is doing something else; as if it were not some rascally trick to secure the throne. . . ."

Thus our talk ran, faster or slower, till we reached the Palace. . . . When we had reached my mistress's rooms . . . Amaranta came in, so much disturbed that she was obliged to wait a little while before she could get over her agitation so far as to explain what was happening. . . .

"It seems that a plot has been discovered to assassinate the King and Queen; everything was ready for a revolt in the Palace."

"How frightful!" exclaimed the diplomate. "I was right in saying that numbers of Jacobins were concealed here under the guise of being his Majesty's servants."

"This has nothing to do with the Jacobins," my mistress went on. "The strangest thing is that the Prince of Asturias is the soul of the conspiracy."

"It is impossible!" said the Marquesa, who was devoted to his Royal Highness. "The Prince is incapable of such a crime. What I said is the exact truth: his enemies have plotted to ruin him by this calumny since they have failed to do so by other means". . . .

"I can but tell you what was told to me. For some time past it has been observed that the Prince passed his evenings shut up alone in his own room where the King and Queen believed him to be engaged in translating a French book. But yesterday his Majesty found a sealed letter in his own room with no address but the words: 'Immediate, immediate, immediate' —

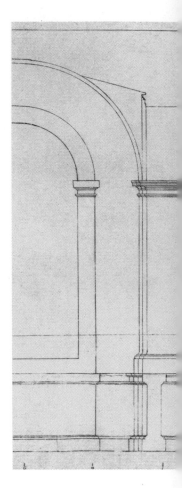

158

The King opened it and read this warning, with no signature: 'Beware! a revolution is brewing in the palace. Peril to the throne; the Queen Maria Louisa is to be poisoned' ". . . .

"You may imagine the state of the poor King. The Prince was immediately suspected, and it was decided to seize his papers. They hesitated for some time as to how to proceed and at length the King determined to search his son's rooms himself. He went thither under pretext of seeking a volume of poems, and, as they say, Don Fernando was so much agitated at seeing him enter that his timid and embarrassed glances guided the King to the spot where the papers were. His Majesty took possession of them all, and it seems that the father and son exchanged some rather strong words, after which Carlos went out in high wrath, ordering the Prince to keep his room without seeing a soul. — This was yesterday. Later on Caballero, the minister, arrived and he and the King examined the papers. What passed at this conference is not known, but it must have been something serious, for the Queen withdrew in tears to her own rooms. Afterwards it was reported that the documents that had fallen into the King's hands contained a clue to fearful schemes, and from what Caballero said after his interview with their Majesties, Prince Ferdinand is to be condemned to death!" . . .

"It would seem that they have determined to have up a regular trial in order to prove who really are the guilty parties," Amaranta went on. "The Prince is to make a declaration to-night before the King."

At this point of these interesting disclosures we heard a noise as of a crowd of people in some place close at hand. As there was not much for me to do in my mistress's rooms, and as curiosity called me forth, I went out and down a staircase which led me into a spacious tapestried hall, opening on both sides into others of equal extent, and decorated in the same manner. I went on through two or three rooms, following the lead of several persons who were making their way to some particular spot; but I saw nothing worthy of note, beyond a few knots of palace attendants whispering together eagerly but mysteriously. . . .

The rooms where I now found myself were the long array of tapestried corridors which extend throughout the inner side of the Palace courts, and serve to connect the royal apartments which look out on the eastern side of the immense structure. I followed with the tide, never considering whether my feet might venture here; and as no one said me nay, I went on unhesitatingly. The halls were but dimly lighted, and in the doubtful gleam the figures of the tapestry looked like shadows clinging to the walls or pale reflections cast by a hidden flame on the dark background. As I walked I glanced at this crowd of mythological beings whose suggestive nakedness decorates the sombre walls built by Philip II, and was about to devote my attention to them more curiously when a strange procession came by which I will attempt to describe.

The Prince of Asturias, who had been formally indicted on a charge of conspiracy, was returning from the King's justice-chamber where he had made his declaration. I shall never forget the details of the melancholy retinue which passed before my astonished eyes and impressed me so vividly that it entirely deprived me of sleep that night. First walked a gentleman holding a large candlestick, as if to light the way, and to this end he carried it high up, though its feeble light only served to make the gold braid glitter on his court suit. Then came a small party of guards, and in their midst a

Detail of the Lower Cloister

159

youth whom I at once recognized, I know not how, as the Crown Prince. He was a well-built lad and ruddy, but his face was not a very pleasant one; the thickness of his black eyebrows and the singular expression of his mouth and high nose were very unattractive, at least to my eyes. He kept his eyes fixed on the ground, and his anxious, gloomy face revealed the bitterness in his soul. By his side was a man of about sixty; at first I did not understand that this could be King Carlos IV, for I had pictured him to myself as a feeble stunted little man; however, as I saw him that night, he was of middle stature, thick-set with a small face and high color, and devoid of any single feature which could suggest a distinction stamped by Nature on his physiognomy between a King of blue blood and a respectable grocer.

My interest centered more on the personages who accompanied the King than on his own royal person; these, as I afterwards learnt, were the ministers and president of the Council. . . . The procession closed with a small detachment of the body-guard and that was all. While the little party went by sepulchral silence reigned all along the way; their footsteps could be heard fainter and fainter, from room to room, till they reached his Highness's apartments. As soon as the royal party had gone in then the buzz of talk began again, and I then saw Amaranta who had come out to look for me, and was speaking to an officer in uniform.

"I believe that in making his declaration his Royal Highness was somewhat disrespectful to the King," said this gentleman.

"So they have made him a prisoner?" asked Amaranta with some interest.

"Yes, Señora. He will be detained in his own room under the eye of sentinels. — You see; here they come again. . . ."

The party were now returning without the Prince, preceded by the gentleman with the candlestick lighting the way. When the King and his ministers had disappeared, the courtiers who had come out into the corridors also vanished into their several quarters, and for some time nothing was to be heard but the slamming of numberless doors. The few lights that had glimmered in these vast precincts were soon extinguished, and the graceful figures on the tapestry faded into darkness like ghosts scared by the crow of the cock to their unknown lurking place.

BENITO PÉREZ GALDÓS
The Court of Charles IV:
A Romance of the Escorial, 1873

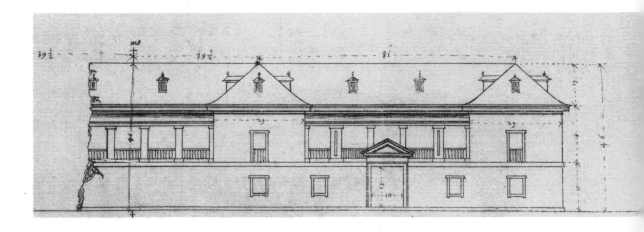

Posterior façade of
the wing of offices

REFERENCE

Chronology of Spanish History

Entries in boldface refer to El Escorial.

1469	Marriage of Ferdinand and Isabella unites Aragon and Castile
1478	Establishment of Spanish Inquisition
1492	Conquest of Granada; Christopher Columbus's first voyage to the New World
1504	Death of Isabella
1506	Brief reign of Philip I; Ferdinand resumes throne
1516	Accession of Charles I, founder of the Spanish Habsburgs
1517	Luther initiates Protestant Reformation
1519	Charles I of Spain elected Holy Roman Emperor, reigns as Charles V
1520–21	*Comunero* uprising
1521	Cortes conquers Mexico
1521–29	Franco-Spanish wars
1527	Birth of Philip II
1533	Pizarro begins conquest of Peru
1540	Ignatius Loyola founds Society of Jesus
1556	Abdication of Charles V; accession of Philip II
1557	**After French defeat at Saint-Quentin, Philip resolves to build El Escorial**
1558	Death of Charles V
1559	**Juan Bautista de Toledo appointed architect of Escorial**
1560	Capital established at Madrid
1562	**Site cleared for Escorial**
1563	**Construction begins**
1565–76	**Philip II deposits manuscript collection in monastery library**
1567	**Juan de Herrera succeeds Juan Bautista de Toledo as architect of Escorial**
1568	Death of Don Carlos, son of Philip II
1569–71	Revolt of the Moriscos
1571	Don Juan defeats Turks at Lepanto
1573	**Royal corpses reinterred at Escorial**
1575	**Design of church of San Lorenzo el Real changed from Latin to Greek cross**
1577	**Lightning strikes belfry, which bursts into flames**
1580	Philip II ascends Portuguese throne
1582	**Completion of church of San Lorenzo**
1584	**Last stone laid at Escorial**
1588	Defeat of the Spanish Armada
1589	**Herrera publishes his treatise on Escorial**
1589–98	War with France
1592	**Library finished**
1595	**Basilica consecrated**
1598	**Philip II dies in royal apartments**
1598	Accession of Philip III
1605	Cervantes publishes *Don Quixote*
1609	Expulsion of the Moriscos
1617	**Philip III begins Pantheon of the Kings**
1618–48	Thirty Years' War
1621	Accession of Philip IV
1640	Philip IV loses Portugal
1640–59	Revolt of the Catalonians
1654	**Completion of Pantheon of the Kings**
1659	Treaty of the Pyrenees ends Spanish ascendancy in Europe
1665	Accession of Charles II
1667–68	War with France over control of Spanish Netherlands
1671	**Fire destroys large part of Escorial, including more than 4,000 manuscripts in monastery library**
1674	Loss of Franche-Comté to France
1684	**Chapel inaugurated**
1700	Accession of Philip V, first of the Spanish Bourbons
1701–14	War of the Spanish Succession
1703	Charles of Austria claims Philip V's throne
1713	Treaty of Utrecht with England and Savoy
1714	Treaty of Rastatt reasserts Philip V's claim to Spanish throne

1724	Abdication of Philip V in favor of his son Louis I; death of Louis and reinstatement of Philip V		1823	Monroe Doctrine discourages further Spanish colonization in South America
1727–29	War with England and France		1824	Bolivia gains independence
1733	**The Escorial Compact signed**		1833	Accession of Isabella II; her mother, Maria Cristina, assumes regency during Isabella's minority
1746	Accession of Ferdinand VI			
1754	Spanish church establishes independence from Rome		1834	Struggle of Ferdinand VII's brother Don Carlos for Spanish throne triggers Carlist War
1756–63	Seven Years' War			
1759	Accession of Charles III		**1837**	**Escorial paintings moved to Madrid as Carlists advance on Segovia**
1762	Treaty of Paris; loss of Minorca and Florida to England			
1767	Jesuits expelled from Spain		1840	Maria Cristina abdicates; Baldomero Espartero assumes regency
1779	Spain sides with colonists in American Revolution		1843	Isabella II comes of age; Ramón Narvaez assumes dictatorial powers
1783	Treaty of Versailles; Spain recovers Florida and Minorca		1854	Leopoldo O'Donnell establishes liberal government
1788	Accession of Charles IV		**1862**	**Pantheon of the Infantes commissioned by Isabella II**
1805	Nelson defeats Franco-Spanish fleet at Trafalgar			
1807	Charles IV abdicates in favor of his son Ferdinand VII; French invade Madrid; Napoleon establishes his brother Joseph as King of Spain		1864	Narvaez named premier, reverts to reactionary policy
			1868	Isabella II flees Spain; Juan Prim establishes liberal provisional government
1808	**Escorial ravaged by French soldiers under La Houssaye**		1871	Amadeo, Duke of Aosta, accepts throne
1812	Wellington defeats French; Joseph abandons Madrid; democratic constitution drawn up at Cadiz		1873	Abdication of Amadeo; First Spanish Republic proclaimed
			1875	Monarchy restored under Alfonso XII
1813	Last of French army retreats from Spain		**1888**	**Maria Cristina, Alfonso's widow, completes Pantheon of the Infantes**
1814	Ferdinand VII restored to Spanish throne			
1819	Loss of Florida to United States; Colombia gains independence		1895	Outbreak of Cuban Revolution
			1898	Spanish-American War
1820	Spaniards under Riego rebel against Ferdinand VII, who reinstates Constitution of 1812 but is imprisoned nonetheless		1902	Accession of Alfonso XIII
			1914–19	World War I; Spain remains neutral
			1936–39	Spanish Civil War; Francisco Franco becomes chief of state
1821	Mexico and Peru gain independence		1939–45	World War II; Spain remains neutral
1823	Battle of the Trocadero; Ferdinand VII restored to power		**1963**	**Extensive repairs completed for fourth centenary**
			1970	Franco names Juan Carlos of Bourbon as his successor

The Spanish Succession: 1469-1931

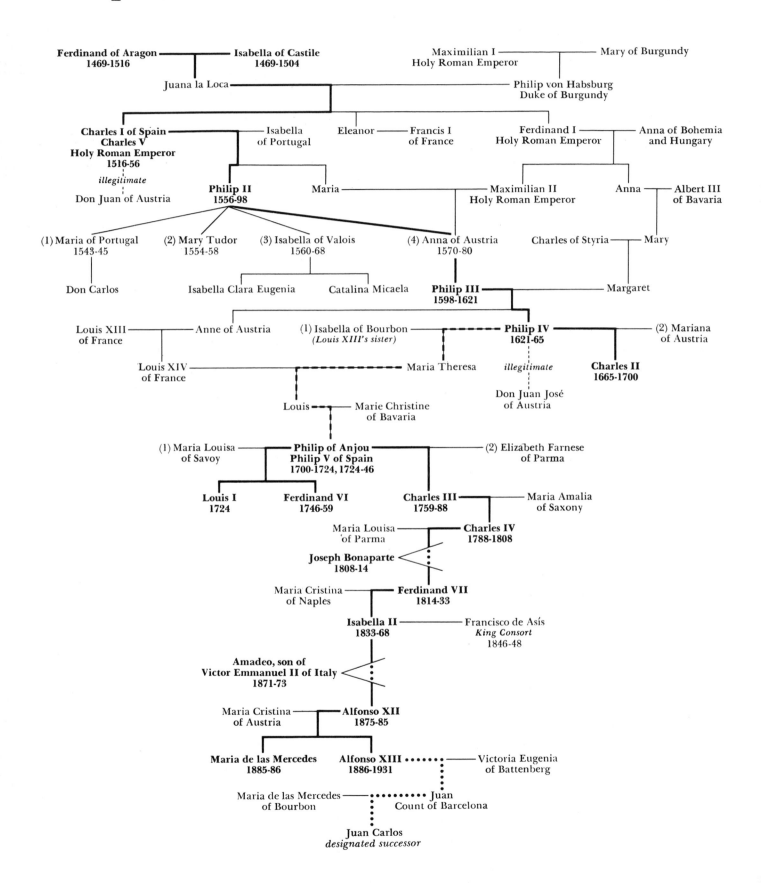

Guide to El Escorial

High in the foothills of the Guadarrama Mountains, some thirty miles northwest of Madrid, stands the imposing structure known as *El Escorial,* the monumental creation of Philip II to the glory of God, man, and the kingdom of Spain.

Although two Spanish architects, Juan Bautista de Toledo and his successor Juan de Herrera, worked on the project, Philip himself was responsible for the general design and he closely supervised the construction. It was conceived in 1557, when Philip resolved to build a monument to Saint Lawrence in gratitude for the Spanish army's victory over the French at Saint-Quentin on the saint's feast day, August 10. The basic structure — laid out in a vast gridiron pattern, perhaps as a symbol of Saint Lawrence's martyrdom by roasting — was completed in twenty-one years, from the laying of the cornerstone in 1563 to the final dedication in 1584. A combination church, monastery, palace, mausoleum, college, and library, the Escorial is almost a city in itself.

The complex, built primarily of gray granite from the nearby mountains, is a giant parallelogram (approximately 680 feet by 500 feet) enclosing a grid-work of halls and courtyards. At the corners are four square, spired towers and in the center, rising above the building, are the twin belfries and the graceful dome of the church. On the east side of the rectangle are the royal apartments, which jut out to form the "handle" of the gridiron. Philip had instructed his architect Herrera: "Above all . . . simplicity in the construction, severity in the whole; nobility without arrogance, majesty without ostentation." And Herrera clearly took heed: the edifice is primarily Doric in style and austerely awesome in effect.

The main entrance, in the center of the west façade, is flanked by Doric half columns and surmounted by the royal shield of Philip II. Above the entrance is a thirteen-foot granite and marble statue of Saint Lawrence, sculpted by Juan Bautista Monegro. Through the entrance is the *Patio of the Kings,* a large courtyard named for statues of the six kings of Judah, also by Monegro, that adorn the façade of the church directly opposite the entrance. To the right of the patio is the convent; to the left, a college that was turned over to the care of Augustinian monks in 1885.

Across the patio is the church of *San Lorenzo el Real,* beloved by Philip above all other buildings in the vast complex. Originally conceived in the shape of a Latin cross, the floor plan of San Lorenzo was modified to a Greek cross. Herrera, who succeeded Juan Bautista upon his death in 1567, oversaw that transformation. Although inspired by St. Peter's Basilica in Rome, the church of San Lorenzo is devoid of the rich ornamentation with which Michelangelo endowed the former. The monumental granite dome, soaring 300 feet above the floor of the church, rests on the unadorned stone connecting arches of four massive piers, relieved of their severity only by some fluted Doric pilasters. The bold vaulting of the nave and aisles, originally covered by plain stucco, was decorated during the reign of Charles II with eight large frescoes by the Neapolitan painter Luca Giordano.

The *High Altar* is separated from the central nave by a low flight of red marble steps. The retable, rising to a height of eighty-six feet, all but fills the wall behind the high altar. Fashioned of precious marbles and gilded bronze, it includes fifteen gilt bronze statues by the Milanese artists Leone and Pompeo Leoni as well as paintings by Pellegrino Tibaldi and Federigo Zuccaro. To the right and left of the altar are gilt bronze royal groups, also by Pompeo Leoni. On one side are the kneeling figures of Philip II; his fourth wife, Anna; his third wife, Isabella; and his first wife, Maria, with their son, Don Carlos. (Philip's second wife, Queen Mary of England, who is buried in Westminster Abbey, is not represented.) On the opposite side, also kneeling in prayer, are Charles V, his empress, Isabella of Portugal, his daughter, Maria, and two of his sisters, Leonora and Maria.

At the west end of the church is the *High Choir,* where Philip II often joined the monastery's Hieronymite monks in their devotions. The 128 choir stalls, all beautifully carved and inlaid with seven different kinds of wood, were designed by Herrera, as was the massive but delicately poised rotating lectern at the front. At one end of the choir is Philip II's stall, which is slightly more commodious than the others and is next to a private door through which he could come and go without disturbing the service. According to popular legend it was here, during vespers, that he was first given word of the victory over the Ottoman Turks at Lepanto. He received the momentous news without a change of expression, merely requesting that a Te Deum be chanted at the end of the service. Since the battle was won in 1571, however, when the church was still in the planning stage, the first part of the story must be discounted. In other particulars the story may be correct; the incident could have occurred in a little church (now part of the cloisters) where the king worshiped during the construction of the main church.

The walls of the choir are decorated with frescoes by Romulo Cincinato and Luca Cambiaso. The latter's *Paradise* (a representation of the Trinity and the Virgin Mary attended by hosts of celestial beings — as well as the artist himself) fills the entire vault.

Adjoining the choir is a small alcove containing a life-size marble *Christ on the Cross* by Benvenuto Cellini, dated 1562, which was presented to Philip II by the Duke of Florence in 1576. It is said that Philip, in the interest of modesty, had a handkerchief tied around the nude figure; the present caretakers have replaced it with a sedate loincloth.

In addition there are libraries in both of the antechoirs containing 221 choir books of uniform size. Each volume is over three feet high and five and a half feet wide when opened, and each was beautifully illuminated in the sixteenth century by two of the monastery's friars and their assistants.

Directly beneath the high altar of the church is the *Pantheon of the Kings,* an octagonal vault some thirty feet in diameter. Planned by Philip II as a tomb for his father, Charles V, and succeeding Spanish kings, it was actually begun by his son, Philip III, in 1617. On his death in 1621, work was suspended, and the neglected crypt began to seep water. The new king, Philip IV, was advised to build the vault elsewhere, but honoring Philip II's wish to have it directly below the altar, he had the crypt drained

and aired, and in 1654 the pantheon was finally completed.

The Pantheon of the Kings is dedicated "to the mortal remains of the Catholic Kings," and, appropriately, almost every Spanish monarch from Charles V on lies there. (Philip V, the first of the Spanish Bourbon line, abhorred the gloomy Escorial and was buried in La Granja; his son Ferdinand VI was buried in Madrid.) Shelved away in tiers of two and four in the walls of the octagon, the royal bodies are carefully segregated — kings (including Isabella II, a queen regnant) on one side, queen mothers of those kings on the other. The tomb, with its gray marble sarcophagi, was a source of macabre fascination to the two last melancholy Habsburgs. Philip IV descended there to pray beside his waiting coffin and once had the sarcophagus of Charles V opened for his inspection (he reported that the corpse, after ninety-six years, was "still perfect"). His son, the feeble-minded Charles II, was fascinated by the mortal remains of his entombed ancestors, and it is said that he too succumbed to the temptation to inspect their coffins. At the sight of the desiccated body of his first wife, Marie Louise, he reputedly collapsed and sank into a deep despair. He died a few years later.

Connected to this vault by a stairway is the *Pantheon of the Infantes,* a series of chambers containing the remains of the lesser royalty — princes, princesses, and those unfortunate queens whose sons died before they could be crowned. This crypt was commissioned by Isabella II in 1862, continued under Alfonso XII, and completed during the regency of his wife, Maria Cristina, in 1888. Philip II's

illegitimate brother, Don Juan of Austria, the hero of Lepanto, also lies here in a marble tomb beneath his handsome effigy. Philip's unbalanced and ill-fated son Don Carlos, who succumbed while imprisoned for plotting his father's overthrow, is buried here.

In the southeast corner of the church is a stairway leading to the *Sacristy,* a long hall to the east of the cloisters noted for its handsome ceiling frescoes by Nicolas Granelo and Fabricio Castello and its richly carved wardrobes containing ecclesiastical vestments. In the center of one wall hangs a silver and rock crystal mirror, a gift of Charles II's mother, Mariana of Austria. At the far end of the sacristy is an altar built by Charles II to house the "relic of the sacred host," a holy wafer presented to Philip II by the Duchess of Navarre in 1592. Above the altar is a painting by Claudio Coello representing the ceremonial displaying of the relic, with Charles II kneeling before the altar. The painting, with its rich detail and deep perspective, is almost a mirror image of the sacristy itself.

Through the porch of the sacristy is an entrance to the *Lower Cloister,* surrounding the *Court of the Evangelists,* a large garden-courtyard named for the white marble statues of the four apostles that have been set in the niches of a small Doric shrine in the center. On the west side of the lower cloister is the grand staircase, an architectural masterpiece by Juan Bautista Castello, the Bergamesco. This broad and graceful sweep of granite leads to the *Upper Cloister,* which is closed to the public. A fresco by Luca Giordano in the well of the staircase commemorates the battle of Saint-Quen-

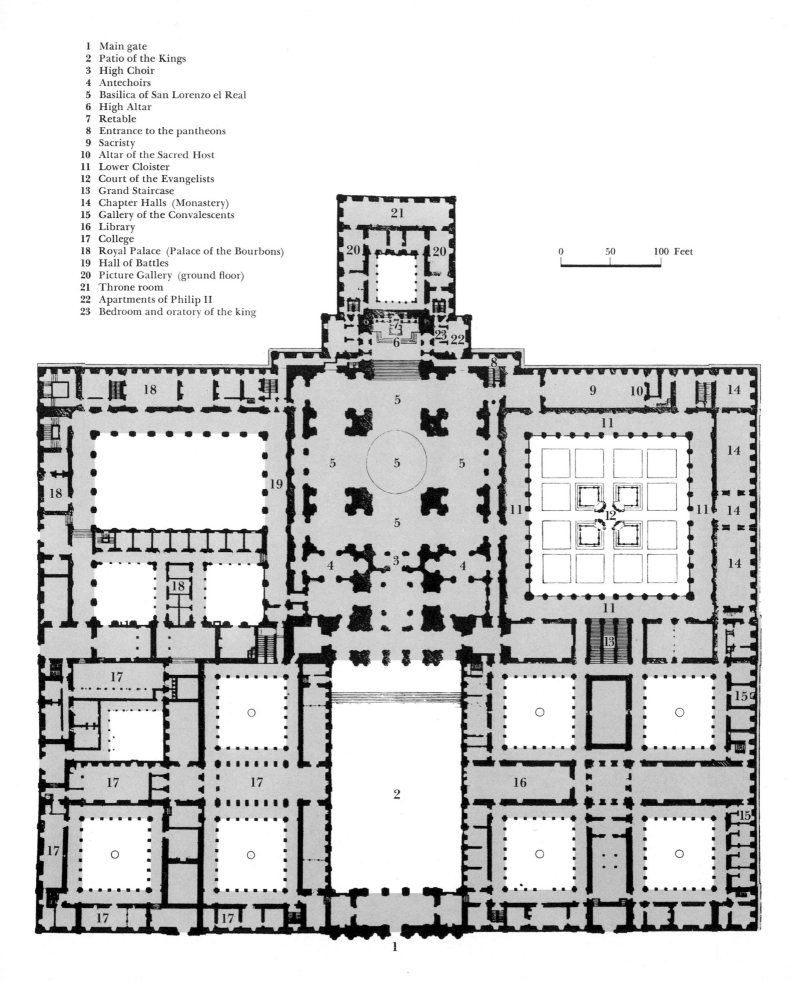

1 Main gate
2 Patio of the Kings
3 High Choir
4 Antechoirs
5 Basilica of San Lorenzo el Real
6 High Altar
7 Retable
8 Entrance to the pantheons
9 Sacristy
10 Altar of the Sacred Host
11 Lower Cloister
12 Court of the Evangelists
13 Grand Staircase
14 Chapter Halls (Monastery)
15 Gallery of the Convalescents
16 Library
17 College
18 Royal Palace (Palace of the Bourbons)
19 Hall of Battles
20 Picture Gallery (ground floor)
21 Throne room
22 Apartments of Philip II
23 Bedroom and oratory of the king

0   50   100 Feet

Study of the door to the kitchen, another sketch by Juan de Herrera

tin. On the south side of the cloisters are the *Chapter Halls,* with ceilings similar to that of the sacristy and paintings by El Mudo (the mute painter who was among Philip II's favorites), Federigo Zuccaro, Luca Giordano, José de Ribera, Annibale Carracci, and others.

In order to see the great masterpieces that once adorned the walls of the sacristy and chapter halls, it is necessary to visit the Escorial's *Picture Gallery.* Among the better-known painters represented there are the Flemish and German masters Bosch, Dürer, Rubens, and Vandyke; the Italians Titian and Tintoretto; and the great Spanish painter Velázquez. One room houses an exquisite Calvary scene by Rogier van der Weyden and El Greco's masterpiece the *Martyrdom of Saint Maurice.* At the end of the picture gallery is the Hall of El Greco, which contains his *Adoration of the Name of Jesus,* in which Philip II figures prominently.

Near the Picture Gallery is an even more recent installation, the *Museum of Architecture,* in which are displayed many of Juan de Herrera's original designs and sketches for the Escorial. Here also are Pierre Perret's engravings of the building, commissioned by Herrera in 1583 to publicize the work under construction. The exhibit includes some of the original tools used by Philip II's workmen and a model of the great crane that Herrera devised to lift the huge granite blocks into place.

Among the greatest treasures of the Escorial is the *Library.* Situated at the west front of the monastery, it is approached by a stairway near the main entrance. The long, vaulted room, lined with cases designed by Herrera, houses one of the finest collections of rare manuscripts in the world and includes some four thousand volumes from Philip's original collection, deposited between 1565 and 1576. In glass display cases down the center of the library are some of the more intriguing rarities: the breviaries of Charles V and Philip II, a fourteenth-century Spanish manuscript of Homer's *Iliad,* and an elaborately illustrated fifteenth-century Apocalypse. The library suffered grave losses in the great fire of 1671 and also during the Napoleonic invasions, but it still contains more than 40,000 books. On the walls of the library are full-length portraits of Charles V, Philip II, Philip III, and Charles II by two seventeenth-century Spanish court painters. The ceiling frescoes, representing the liberal arts, are by Pellegrino Tibaldi.

In the northeast section of the Escorial, occupying almost the entire quadrant, is the *Royal Palace,* entered through a portal in the north façade. In contrast to the simplicity of the rest of the Escorial, the palace (never occupied by Philip II) was richly decorated by a succession of Spanish Bourbons, who used it intermittently as a summer residence and royal retreat.

Charles III was the first to refurbish the palace after its fall from favor during the reign of Philip V. Charles's love of hunting drew him to the abundant game around the Escorial, and he and his son Charles IV, who shared his passion, restored the palace to its former splendor. Rich tapestries — five by Goya depicting typical Spanish scenes and diversions — adorn the walls, and one of the ceilings is elaborately painted in Pompeian style.

Adjoining the palace rooms is the *Hall of Battles,* where a spectacular, 177-foot-long fresco that covers an entire wall details the victory of the Castilians over the Moors in the battle of Higueruela in 1431. In the same hall are frescoes of the battle of Saint-Quentin and of the Spanish fleet's expeditions to the Azores.

A narrow stairway leads to the *Private Apartments of Philip II,* the unpretentious chambers of the founder and his family. Neglected and vacant during the eighteenth and nineteenth centuries, they were restored at the beginning of the twentieth with faithful reproductions and whatever original furniture and personal possessions had survived. Among the latter are a clavichord of Charles V and the chair in which Philip II was carried from Madrid on his last journey to the Escorial.

The royal apartments are divided into three sections — the family quarters, the throne room (where Philip II conducted audiences in an atmosphere of almost arrogant simplicity), and the king's private rooms, consisting only of an antechamber, a study, and a bedroom connected to a small altar room. The original furnishings of his study — a writing desk, bookstand, some straight-backed armchairs, and a small chair on which to rest his infected leg — bear witness to the modesty of the king's personal demands. The small altar room has an aperture overlooking the high altar, an opening through which the bedridden Philip II could hear mass during his final, agonizing illness. On September 13, 1598, the monarch died; his last breath was drawn a few yards from the high altar of the church — the heart of the Escorial he loved so well.

Selected Bibliography

Brandi, Karl. *The Emperor Charles V*. Translated by C. V. Wedgwood. London: Jonathan Cape Ltd., 1968.

Brenan, Gerald. *The Spanish Labyrinth*. New York: Cambridge University Press, 1960.

Davies, R. Trevor. *The Golden Century of Spain: 1501-1621*. New York: St. Martin's Press, 1954.

Elliott, J. H. *Imperial Spain: 1649-1716*. New York: St. Martin's Press, 1964.

————. *The Revolt of the Catalans*. Cambridge: Cambridge University Press, 1963.

Froude, J. A. *The Spanish Story of the Armada*. New York: Charles Scribner's Sons, 1892.

Kamen, Henry. *The Spanish Inquisition*. London: Weidenfeld & Nicolson, Ltd., 1965.

Lynch, John. *Spain Under the Habsburgs*. 2 vols. New York: Oxford University Press, 1964-69.

Mattingly, Garrett. *The Armada*. Boston: Houghton Mifflin Co., 1959.

Parry, J. H. *The Spanish Seaborne Empire*. New York: Alfred A. Knopf, Inc., 1966.

Patrimonio Nacional. *El Escorial*. 2 vols. Madrid: Ediciones Patrimonio Nacional, 1963.

Petrie, Charles A. *Philip II of Spain*. New York: W. W. Norton & Co., 1963.

Prescott, William Hickling. *History of the Reign of Philip II*. 3 vols. Philadelphia: J. B. Lippincott Co., 1916.

Smith, Bradley. *Spain — A History in Art*. New York: Simon and Schuster, Inc., 1966.

Acknowledgments and Picture Credits

The Editors make grateful acknowledgment for the use of excerpted material from the following works:

A Romantic in Spain by Théophile Gautier. Translated by Catherine Alison Phillips. Copyright 1926 and renewed 1954 by Alfred A. Knopf, Inc. The excerpt appearing on page 138 is reproduced by permission of Alfred A. Knopf, Inc.

A Sampler of Castile by Roger Eliot Fry. Copyright 1923 by Roger Fry. The excerpt appearing on pages 148–49 is reproduced by permission of Mrs. Pamela Diamand and Hogarth Press.

Adventures in Spain by Alexandre Dumas. Translated by Alma Elizabeth Murchison. Copyright 1959 by Alma Elizabeth Murchison. The excerpt appearing on page 139 is reproduced by permission of Peter Owen Ltd.

Familiar Spanish Travels by William Dean Howells. Copyright 1940 by John Mead Howells and Mildred Howells. The excerpt appearing on pages 147–48 is reproduced by permission of W. W. Howells.

Iberia by James A. Michener. Copyright 1968 by Random House, Inc. The excerpt appearing on page 134 is reproduced by permission of Random House, Inc.

Philip II of Spain by Sir Charles A. Petrie. Copyright 1963 by Sir Charles A. Petrie. The excerpt appearing on page 92 is reproduced by permission of Curtis Brown Ltd. on behalf of Sir Charles A. Petrie.

Spain by Nikos Kazantzakis. Copyright 1963 by Nikos Kazantzakis. The excerpt appearing on page 150 is reproduced by permission of Simon and Schuster, Inc. and William Morris Agency on behalf of the estate of Nikos Kazantzakis.

The Armada by Garrett Mattingly. Copyright 1959 by Garrett Mattingly. The excerpt appearing on pages 146–47 is reproduced by permission of Houghton Mifflin Co. and Jonathan Cape Ltd.

The Editors would like to express their particular appreciation to the Patrimonio Nacional in Madrid for its generous cooperation, to Michael Holford in London for his creative photography, and to Jane de Cabanyes in Madrid and George Vasquez at the University of Maryland for their invaluable assistance. In addition the Editors would like to thank the following organizations and individuals:

El Escorial — Fray Gregorio Andrés Martinez, Anselmo Paldos, Eusebio Saez Rodrigo, Amelia Herranz García

Marilyn Flaig, New York

Nancy J. Kelly, New York

Kate Lewin, Paris

Ministerio de Asuntos Exteriores, Madrid — Manuel María de Barandica y Uhagón, José-Vicente Torrente Secórun

Museo del Prado, Madrid — Xavier de Salas

Patrimonio Nacional, Madrid — Fernando Fuertes de Villavicencio, Angel Oliveras Guart

Spanish Consulate General, New York — Alberto Oliva, Antonio Serrano

Spanish National Tourist Office, New York — Antonio Alonso

The title or description of each picture appears after the page number (boldface), followed by its location. Photographic credits appear in parentheses. The following abbreviations are used:

E(MH) — El Escorial (Michael Holford)
P(MH) — Museo del Prado (Michael Holford)
P(DMM) — Museo del Prado (David Manso Martin)

and right, Engravings of a penitent and a heretic, from *Historia Inquisitionis* by P. van Limborch, 1692. The British Museum **92** Medallion of Queen Elizabeth I, 1588. The British Museum **93** Four English playing cards depicting the defeat of the Spanish Armada, 17th century. All, National Maritime Museum, Greenwich **94-95** Detail of an anonymous painting of the launch of the English fireships. National Maritime Museum, Greenwich **95** Engraving of the fleets off Portland Bill by Augustine Ryther, from *Expeditionis Hispanorum* by Petruccio Ubaldini, 1590. The British Museum **97** Anonymous Flemish painting of a political allegory, 1590. Brigadier D. S. Schreiber **98** Vestment made for Philip II's funeral. E(MH) **100** Portrait of Philip II by Juan Pantoja de la Cruz, 1598. El Escorial (David Manso Martin) **101** The High Altar seen·from the bedroom of Philip II at El Escorial (Michael Holford)

CHAPTER VI **104** Portrait of Philip III attributed to Diego Rodriguez de Silva y Velázquez. P(DMM) **105** Portrait of Philip IV by Velázquez. P(DMM) **107** Painting of deer hunting at Aranjuez by Juan Bautista Martinez del Mazo, 1665. P(MH) **108** *Las Meninas* by Velázquez, 1656. P(DMM) **109** The *Surrender of Breda* by Velázquez, 1635. P(DMM) **110** Drawing of the mummy of Emperor Charles V by Vicente Palmaroli, c. 1870 (Ruiz Vernacci, Madrid) **111** Portrait of Charles II by Juan Carreno de Miranda. P(MH) **112** Altar painting of *The Sacred Form* by Claudio Coello in the sacristy of El Escorial (Michael Holford) **114-15** Anonymous painting of El Escorial in flames, 1671. School of Architecture, Madrid (Oronoz) **118-19** The Pantheon of the Kings at El Escorial (Michael Holford)

CHAPTER VII **122** Portrait of Charles III by Francisco José de Goya y Lucientes. P(DMM) **123** *The Family of Charles IV* by Goya, 1808. P(DMM) **124** Etching from *Disasters of War* by Goya, 1814. Metropolitan Museum of Art, Rogers Fund, 1922 **125** Etching from *Disasters of War* by Goya, 1814. Metropolitan Museum of Art, Bequest of Michael Dreicer, 1921 **126-27** *The Third of May, 1808* by Goya, 1814. P(DMM) **128** Detail of painting *Jura de la Constitución por Isabel II* by Josea Castelard y Perea. Museo Municipal, Madrid (Oronoz) **130** Cartoon of *The Ball of San Antonio de la Florida* by Goya. P(DMM) **131** Tapestry of *The Kite* by Goya, 1778, in the Palace of the Bourbons at El Escorial (Michael Holford) **134-35** *Philip V, Conqueror of Heresy* attributed to Felipe de Silva, 18th century. E (MH)

EL ESCORIAL IN LITERATURE **136** Gouache of monks in the library from *Catalogo de Manuscritos de El Escorial por el Padre Juan de Cuenca*, 18th century. E(MH) H-II-3, fol 2 **138-60** Fourteen architectural drawings from *Trazas de Juan de Herrera . . . para el Monasterio del Escorial*. Biblioteca de Palacio, Madrid

REFERENCE **168** Architectural drawing from *Trazas de Juan de Herrera . . . para el Monasterio del Escorial*. Biblioteca de Palacio, Madrid

Index